D1242232

Map of Louisiana as it appeared in *Harper's History of the Great Rebellion.* (September, 1863)

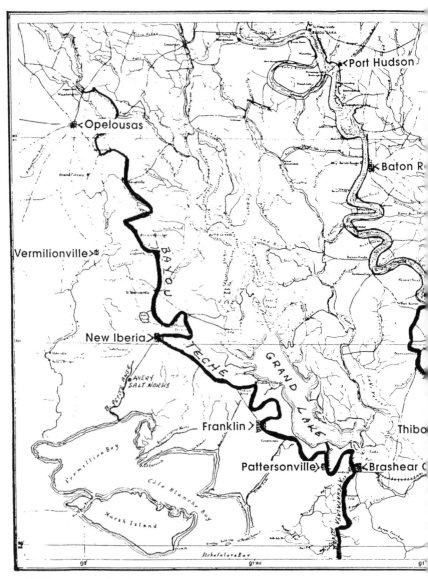

Wide area map showing a large portion of South Louisiana. The original
map was touched up by the author to show more clearly the location of

A GUNBOAT
NAMED *DIANA*

by Morris Raphael

Morris Raphael

HARLO   DETROIT

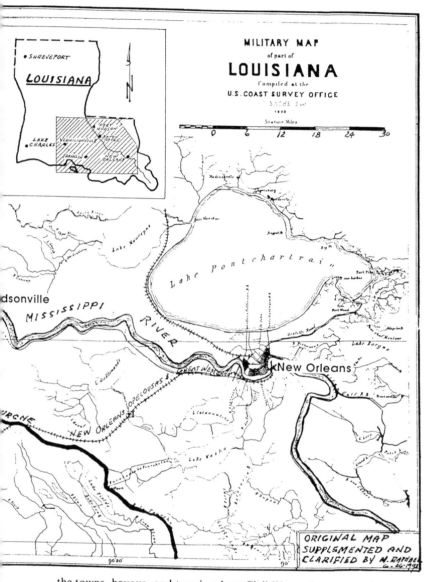

the towns, bayous, and terrain where Civil War action occurred.

OTHER BOOKS BY THE SAME AUTHOR:

The Battle in the Bayou Country
ISBN 0-9608866-0-5

Weeks Hall—The Master of the Shadows
ISBN 0-9608866-1-3

The Weeks Hall Tapes
ISBN 0-9608866-2-1

How Do You Know When You're in Acadiana?
ISBN 0-9608866-3-x

Mystic Bayou
ISBN 0-9608866-4-8

Murder on the Teche Queen
ISBN 0-9608866-5-6

Halo for a Devil
ISBN 0-9608866-6-4

The Loup-Garou of Côte Gelée
ISBN 0-9608866-7-2

Maria—Goddess of the Teche
ISBN 0-9608866-8-0

Any of the above books may be ordered from
Morris Raphael Books, the sole distributor.

A Gunboat
Named *Diana*

For

G.K. Pratt Munson

Soldiers fought in bloody conflict
Along this hallowed shore
But the *Diana* and troops are silent
They are gone forevermore.

(A verse from Morris Raphael's poem
The Voice of the Diana.)

CONTENTS

ACKNOWLEDGMENTS

In the course of writing a book that requires documentation and specific material, an author often finds himself at the mercy and kindness of many people and institutions. Without their help, all the years of research and writing would hardly bring about the ultimate success that he is seeking.

I've been fortunate that so many have helped—some went the extra mile. Mrs. Peggy Fox, who is executive secretary at the Harold B. Simpson Confederate Research Center at Hillsboro, Texas, kept me abreast of anything she found that referred to the *Diana*. Through the efforts of my U.S. Representative, Billy Tauzin, I was able to secure the cooperation of the Library of Congress, the Smithsonian Institution, and other archives. He was very helpful.

Mrs. Routh Wilby of Franklin was very considerate in allowing me the use of her precious papers and maps, which gave my book a fitting climax. (An account of her contributions are found in the epilogue.)

It's amazing how writing brings about friendships that one would never have otherwise. Two that come to mind are Will Molineux of Williamsburg, Virginia, and L. Boyd Finch of Tucson, Arizona. Will, who is editorial page editor of the

15

Newport News, is the great-grandson of Colonel Edward Molineux who courageously led the 159th New York and was wounded at the battle of Irish Bend. Boyd, historian and author, is in the process of publishing a book on Confederate Major Sherod Hunter, who commanded the daring recapture of Brashear City. Both of these gentlemen supplied me with exclusive information.

Other acknowledgments include: Mrs. Catherine Dilsaver, curator at the Morgan City, Louisiana, museum, has always been cooperative; Bruce Turner, head of Archives at the University of Southwestern Louisiana at Lafayette, has been generous with his assistance; my good friend Pratt Munson of New Iberia has constantly encouraged me and aided me in my photographic needs; and thanks to my son John for the index.

Contacts which proved beneficial were: the University of Wisconsin at River Falls; the State Historical Society of Wisconsin; the Mariner's Museum, Newport News, Virginia; Confederate Naval Museum, Columbus, Georgia; University of Texas, Austin; Rosenburg Library, Galveston, Texas; Department of the Navy, Washington, D.C.; John Moroz, Jr., researcher, Arlington, Virginia; James Shumer, USAF, Thomaston, Georgia; Jim Mundie, author, Houston, Texas; Major Warren Farr, San Antonio, Texas; Ms. C.J. Houston, Coppel, Texas; Mrs. Marion Dukes, Atlanta, Georgia; M. C. Rose, Franklin, Louisiana; Jim Hopkins, Houston, Texas; and many, many more. My sincere thanks go out to all these fine people.

Last, but certainly not least, a special thanks to my dear wife Helen, who has endured the trials and tribulations of an author who has struggled through ten books. She deserves a gold medal as big as the moon. Her critiquing, proofreading, good judgment, and patience are deeply appreciated.

FOREWORD

The mid-1800s was perhaps the most romantic period in South Louisiana history. There were plantations, mansions, balls, chivalry. cottonspinning, and sugarmaking. Steamboats plowing through the rivers and bayous always seemed to be a big attraction. It was not unusual to see field hands and overseers alike gathering along the banks, gazing and waving at a steam-powered vessel until it gradually disappeared around the bend.

Although steamers were a main mode of transportation in those days, they were not only engaged in hauling supplies and passengers but were equipped for entertainment as well. Stage shows, picnics, bars, and gambling were quite common, and to accompany your loved one on a midnight cruise was regarded as a most enjoyable experience.

Because of the popularity of the steamboat, some took on intriguing names such as *Empress, Queen of the West, Will of the Wisp, Princess,* and of course, the *Diana.*

But as the 1860s rolled around, the war triggered a grim transfiguration: Dissension and misery prevailed; plantations were turned into battlefields; mansions were destroyed, sacked or occupied by troops; and the pleasurable steamers were converted into troop transports and gunboats.

17

In the chapters to come, the author endeavors to tell of the unusual experiences of the *Diana* and at the same time bring out some of the dramatic history of the conflict as it happened in South Louisiana.

But writing this book was certainly not an easy task. Apparently there were at least four vessels named *Diana* which were active along the lower Mississippi River and Gulf Coast areas, servicing such port cities as New Orleans, Mobile, Galveston, and Houston.

In an effort to obtain the history and background of my subject vessel, the real *Diana* which was so prominent in the Teche campaign, I began contacting archivists across the nation. Most were cooperative and tried to help, but were unable to furnish me with the information I needed.

In 1988, a letter by Mr. Harold Langley, curator of Naval History at the Smithsonian Institution, Washington, D.C., explained why so little data was available. One of their staff members, the late Earl Geoghegan, who devoted many years to researching the Confederate Navy and blockade runners, remarked in his notes that most of the records of these ships were destroyed by fire when Richmond fell to the Union forces.

But these disappointments didn't deter me. I rolled up my sleeves, got into the trenches, absorbing as much as I possibly could from the Official Records of the Army and Navy, regimental histories, diaries, letters, newspapers, and Civil War magazines. Eventually, things began to break as pertinent information began to funnel in from some of my fine friends and museum contacts. (They are noted in the acknowledgments.)

But just when I thought I had the right *Diana* "nailed

down," more frustration entered the picture. According to the enrollment record in 1858, the vessel was owned by three Houston men, John H. Sterrett, B.A. Shepherd, and F.W. Smith. But, much to my dismay, I found out later that a Confederate vessel by the same name, which was originally owned by the same three men, was captured by the Yankees near Houston in 1865. This vessel was found sinking and abandoned by the Rebels. This was a real let-down. I was baffled, because the *Diana* I was writing about was scuttled in 1863 near Franklin, Louisiana.

I agonized until Mrs. Peggy Fox, a Texas archivist, sent me some papers which solved the problem. The Houston Navigation Co. of Sterret, Shepherd and Smith, had at one time owned two vessels named *Diana* which were operating in different sectors. The *Diana* in the Teche campaign was a side-wheel steamer transport which was converted into a gunboat, while the other was a stern-wheel steamer that was transformed into a ram.

In the epilogue of this book may be found a generous account of Mrs. Routh Wilby's findings which solves another mystery.

Should the reader desire a more detailed account of the action, it is suggested that he follow up on the sources found in the references, and also read my book *The Battle in the Bayou Country* which was published in 1975.

I hope you find *A Gunboat Named Diana* interesting, informative and entertaining. It was designed for your reading pleasure.

Morris Raphael

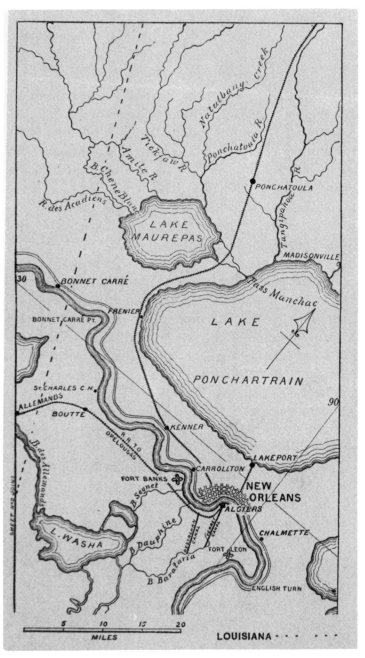

Map of the New Orleans area. (From Irwin's *19th Army Corps*.)

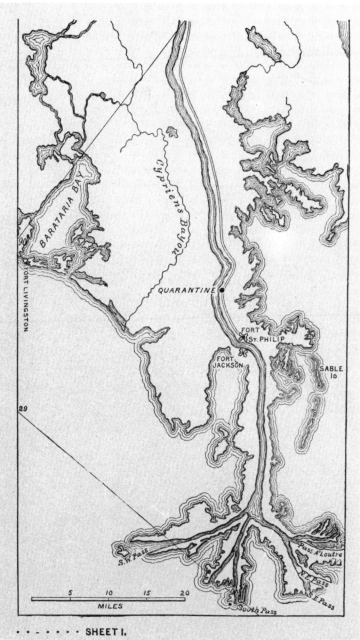

Forts at lower end of the Mississippi River. (From Irwin's *19th Army Corps.)*

Chapter 1

THE INVASION

IT WAS SPRINGTIME IN DIXIE. THE YEAR WAS 1862 and the War Between the States was now in full swing. The usual tranquility of the season was being shattered by bloody fighting and widespread destruction as a powerful Yankee invasion gradually penetrated to the deep South.

The Union command had already established an effective Gulf Coast blockade and was busy mapping its strategy to capture New Orleans which was looked upon as the "Gibraltar of the South." A victory here would give the Federals an ideal base for clearing out the Rebel strongholds along the Mississippi River and facilitate the Union shipment of troops and supplies. It would also split the Confederacy and cut off transportation of food and armament.

New Orleans was by far the largest and richest city in the South, having a population of approximately 170,000 persons. The value of shipments from the Crescent City docks during the year 1860-1861 was recorded as being $25 million in sugar and $92 million in cotton. The export trade in these two items alone was larger than any other city in the world.[1]

Nearly 2,000 sailing vessels and steamers were engaged in the transport of various products at this busy Mississippi River port. An innumerable number of river and bayou steamers constantly lined the city wharves adjacent to the shops, warehouses and factories. The Confederates looked upon this flotilla as a mighty military weapon to be used whenever the need arose.[2]

The Confederate command as well as the citizens of New Orleans shared a common feeling that New Orleans was impregnable to attack by way of the Mississippi River.[3] This opinion was supported by the fact that two mighty forts were located about seventy miles downstream of the city and about thirty miles upstream from the river's mouth. Fort Jackson on the western bank was a five-sided work of immense strength mounting seventy guns, while across the river and a few hundred yards upstream stood Fort St. Philip. Although this fort was of inferior strength, it mounted forty guns and was flanked by two strong batteries.

In summing up the strength, one observer noted that the forts with their outer works pointed one hundred twenty-eight heavy guns upon the river and that fourteen of these guns could be operated under cover. The batteries were protected by ditches wide and deep, by walls of immense strength, by bulwarks of earth and sod, and by enfilading howitzers.[4]

These two fortifications had been previously constructed and strengthened by the United States Government at a cost of $1.25 million as a means of defending the river against foreign enemies. Ironically these bastions had fallen into the hands of its domestic enemy—the Confederacy.[5]

Confederate Major General Mansfield Lovell was in

command of the land units which protected the vast New Orleans area, but his forces only numbered around 5,000. Lovell placed Brigadier General Johnson K. Duncan, a Pennsylvanian who was educated at West Point, in command of the entire exterior line of defense. Duncan was assisted by Lt. Colonel Ed Higgins who was once an officer of the United States and placed in charge of both Fort Jackson and Fort St. Philip. According to a Union historian there were 1,500 troops garrisoned at the two forts.[6]

Above the forts lay a Confederate fleet of fifteen armed vessels, including an iron ram and a huge floating battery called the *Louisiana*.[7] This vessel was built upon the hull of a dry dock, propelled by four engines, and armed with sixteen guns. However, it was still in an unfinished state and the Rebels were trying desperately to complete it before the expected attack.[8]

As an added defense measure, the Confederates constructed a floating obstruction which extended across the river near the forts. At first, this barrier was made of logs fastened by shackles end to end. But floating timber, brush, and other debris piled upon the upstream side of the chain, plus the pressure generated by the mighty Mississippi River current and strong winds, caused the chain to break.

Lt. Colonel Higgins, however, designed a new barrier. He had several schooners brought to the same location and had them anchored thirty yards apart with bows upstream. Heavy chains which had been obtained from Pensacola and Norfolk navy yards were fastened together into one long cable. One end of this was made fast on shore and carried across the schooners from one to the other where the chain was securely fastened and then tied to the other bank. The

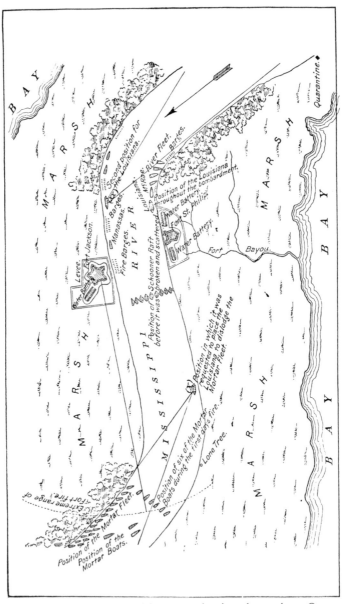

Diagram showing location of forts, naval units, obstructions, Quarantine station, and general terrain along the lower Mississippi River during the latter part of April, 1862. (From the *Official Records of the Union and Confederate Navies*, Series 1, Volume 18.)

supported chain allowed the driftwood floating down the river to run between the schooners without any resistance. Rigging, ratlines, and cable were left to trail astern of the schooners as an additional impediment to tangle into the propeller wheels of the invaders.[9]

On February 23, 1862, Union Major General Benjamin Butler was placed in command of the Department of the Gulf and assigned the task of capturing the city of New Orleans. On March 20, he arrived at Ship Island which is located off the Mississippi Gulf Coast and before long collected a ground force of about 13,500 troops.[10] Flag Officer David Farragut, aboard the Union sloop of war *Hartford,* had been placed in command of the West Gulf Squadron and the naval portion of the expedition destined for the reduction of the Crescent City.[11] Farragut's fleet consisted of seventeen vessels mounting 154 guns. Four were screw-sloops, one a side-steamer, three screw-corvettes, and nine screw-gunboats. Assigned to this fleet were twenty mortar boats under the command of Captain David Porter.[12]

The plan was for Captain Porter, with his fleet, to anchor below the forts and fire continuously upon them until they were reduced or until Porter's ammunition was nearly exhausted. If this bombardment proved to be unsuccessful, then Captain Farragut would attempt to run the gauntlet of the two forts. Should Farragut succeed in this action, he would clear the river of the Confederate fleet, cutting off the forts from their supplies and then push on at least to reconnoiter the next obstruction. After Farragut had passed the forts, General Butler would take his troops via the Gulf of Mexico to the rear of Fort St. Philip, land his troops in the swamps there and attempt to capture the fort by assault.

First day's bombardment of Forts Jackson and St. Philip by Federal schooners. (From a sketch by William Waud aboard the *Mississippi*.)

The Confederates had made no preparations to resist an attack from this direction, supposing the swamps impassable, and consequently, mounted no heavy guns to the rear of Fort St. Philip.[13] Laying the groundwork for this Union strategy was Lt. Godfrey Weitzel, Butler's chief engineer who had worked on the forts two years prior to the war. Lt. Weitzel, a six-foot-four-inch West Pointer, had hunted ducks in these swamps and assured Butler that the landing of troops there would be difficult, but not impossible.[14]

Weitzel also informed the Union command that the guns which protected the forts were inferior. He pointed out that all of them were the old smooth-bore guns picked up at the different works around the city with the exception of about six ten-inch columbiads and two 100-pound rifled guns. He contended that if the forts had been provided with the full compliment of the best modern artillery, it would be impossible for wooden ships to succeed in the attack.[15]

On the 18th of April, Porter's mortar fleet opened fire on the two forts. Although considerable damage was done as the result of incessant bombardment, it became apparent that success was not to be attained in this action alone. On April 20, Farragut, determined to pass the forts with his fleet, ordered the gunboats *Pinola* and *Itasca* to provide an opening in the chain barrier.[16]

That night, the *Pinola* was to blow up one of the chain supporting hulks by means of electrically-fired torpedoes while the crew of the *Itasca* was to board the next schooner, cut the chain and also the cable by which the vessel was anchored. Then, when the schooner would swing free with the current, it would leave an opening of about 180 feet.

Although the *Pinola* made its way to the schooner, the

Shown are members of a Union naval crew engaged in the breaking of the chain barrier which extended across the Mississippi River below the forts, and which were supported by hulks. (The University of Texas Library at Austin.)

petard did not explode because the swift current and wind caused the *Pinola* to back off downstream, breaking the electric connection. However, the *Itasca* managed to make fast to the next schooner which was located near the middle of the river, and although both forts detected the activity and commenced firing, the crew of the *Itasca* worked in the safety of the darkness and smoke. The chain was cut with sledge and chisel, and the cable that anchored the hulk was slipped. But the current and wind were so great that the *Itasca* and the schooner, along with the chain, were swung into the eastern shore under the fire of both forts. Here, the *Itasca* was grounded in the mud hard and fast, but the *Pinola* dashed to the rescue and, after an hour's tugging, managed to free her sister gunboat from her perilous position, although both vessels were showered with shot and shell.[17]

Even though the invaders had produced a wide gap in the chain barrier, the Confederates had an "ace in the hole." They had converted some of the immense flat boats into fire rafts as additional protection. These units were around 200-feet long, forty-feet wide, six-feet deep, and had been primarily used in the transport of coal along the Mississippi. The Rebels filled these boats with light wood and cotton which were afterwards saturated with pitch and turpentine.

The Rebels "put the torch" to one of these rafts as it was directed through the chain opening. Powered by the swift current, the raft passed within fifty feet of Farragut's flagship, the *Hartford,* scorching some of the men and grazed another Union gunboat. The mortar boatsmen finally grappled the fiery menace, towed it to shore and put out the fire.[18]

After four days bombardment and 4,000 shells had been expended by the Union Navy, it was apparent that the Rebels

Union Flag Officer David Farragut.

Union General Benjamin Butler.

had not been severely weakened as they returned a steady fire from both sides of the river. Buildings were demolished, levees destroyed, and many of the Confederates were killed and mangled, but they managed to hold out.[19]

On the sixth day, Porter's bombardment had slowed down somewhat and fire from the forts had stopped altogether. Farragut now decided to make his big move. He had issued general orders in preparation of the invasion which included that vessels be loaded more at the bow so that if the boat touched bottom it would not swing head-down the river. Also, light Jacob's ladders were to be made to throw over the sides for the use of carpenters in sealing shot-holes. Tubs of water were ordered on deck for the purpose of extinguishing fires and also for drinking. The crew was to provide a "kedge in the mizzen chains on the quarter, with a hawser bent and leading through the stern chock, ready for any emergency. Also grapnels in boats ready to tow off fire ships." Since the attack was to be at night, he ordered the decks of the boats painted white in order to facilitate the crew's detection of objects. All spare chains were hung up and down the sides of vessels at vital locations for the protection of machinery from enemy gunfire.[20]

The attack was scheduled for the following day, April 24, at 3:30 a.m., just before moonrise. Two red lanterns displayed at the peak of the flagship at two o'clock gave the signal for action, and at half-past three, the whole fleet was in action.[21] The vicious gunfire which erupted from both sides was described by Major Joseph Bell, who was Butler's staff officer, as being like all the earthquakes in the world and all the thunder and lightning storms going off at the same time within a space of two miles.[22]

Artist's view of the capture of Forts Jackson and St. Phillip on April 24, 1862, by the fleet of Union Flag Officer David Farragut. The Rebel gunboats and rams were destroyed or captured during the seven day battle. (National Archives)

Although Farragut had divided his fleet into five divisions and arranged for an orderly attack, his plan was somewhat abandoned because of the confusion of battle, the deafening noises, the darkness itself, and individual battles with gunboats. The mortar boats remained in place, aiding in the attack with rapid fire, while most of the Federal fleet was making its passage between the Rebel gauntlet of guns. The fire rafts were having a telling effect upon the invaders, as one caused the *Hartford* to go aground. The *Mosher,* a Confederate unarmed tug, shoved one of the blazing rafts against the helpless *Hartford,* causing considerable damage. The *Mosher* was then sunk by a broadside shot from a Yankee gunboat, and the *Hartford,* after extinguishing its fire, worked its way free to resume the shelling of the forts.[23]

When the sun rose, Farragut found himself and all but four of his fleet above the forts. The *Itasca, Winona,* and *Kennebec* were disabled and withdrawn from action, while the *Varuna* was sunk by Confederate gunboats. Nearly all of the Rebel gunboats were destroyed, the fire rafts had been overcome, and the gunners at the forts had been driven from their positions.[24] The Rebel floating fortress, the *Louisiana,* was still in an unfinished state, but was moved near Fort St. Philip and given a crew of 150 men.[25] She was stationed near two other gunboat survivors, the *McRae* and the *Defiance.* The C.S.S. *McRae,* which had gathered the wounded from both forts, was granted permission by the Yankees to proceed to New Orleans under a flag of truce.[26] Later, the *Louisiana* and *Defiance* were scuttled to avoid being captured by Farragut's fleet.[27]

General Butler had left three regiments at the mouth of the river and brought the rest of the force to Sable Island in

The Quarantine complex, which included the U.S. Government hospital and store-houses, was located about two miles upriver from Forts Jackson and St. Philip. The recapture of Quarantine represented the first government property recovered by Federal forces in Louisiana. The small house on the left was the temporary headquarters of Union General Benjamin Butler. (*Frank Leslie's Illustrated Newspaper*, June 14, 1862)

the rear of Fort St. Philip. Several regiments made their way through a small canal to Quarantine, which was six miles above Fort St. Philip, cutting off any escape attempts by the Rebels at that point. (Quarantine was a U.S. Government station that included an office, hospital, and storehouse.) However, at half-past two on the afternoon of April 28, the Confederate flags over Forts Jackson and St. Philip were taken down and replaced with U.S. flags. Soon it became known that Duncan had surrendered to Porter and the three Union regiments at the passes were transported upriver to take over occupation of the forts.[28]

In spite of the ferocity of battle between the naval fleets, the continuous bombardment of the forts, and the heavy gunfire from the batteries, casualties were surprisingly low. The Union navy had only 39 killed and 71 wounded, while the Confederates at the forts lost only 11 killed and 39 wounded. Losses aboard the Rebel and "state" ships numbered around 74 killed and a like number injured. The Confederate gunboat *Governor Moore,* which was trapped upriver by 7 Union gunboats near Camp Chalmette, was riddled with shot and shell and finally scuttled. There were 57 fatalities on this ship alone.[29]

Farragut, who had become a Union hero overnight, sped upriver with a portion of his fleet, examining Rebel strongpoints, and confiscating the steamboats' valuable equipment, materials, and food stuffs. He even destroyed guns at a fort above the city.[30] But the Confederates did their best to destroy everything that they felt would be of use to the victorious invaders. They put the torch to 15,000 bales of cotton, heaps of coal and wood, dry docks, and a large number of steamboats. They even broke barrels of molasses and

37

The Confederate Steamer *Governor Moore*, trapped and shelled by seven Union gunboats near Chalmette, suffered 57 fatalities. *(Official Records of the Union and Confederate Navies)*

sugar. The poor people were reported to be carrying away sugar in their baskets and aprons.[31]

Farragut then sent 250 marines into New Orleans to take formal possession of the city and to guard the public buildings until the U.S. Army officially took over.[32]

According to Confederate Commander John K. Mitchell, only a handful of Confederate vessels survived the Union onslaught at the forts and he believed that there were only two which managed to escape to the city. They were the gunboat *Jackson* and the transport *Diana*.[33] But the freedom of the *Diana* was short-lived because on April 27 she was captured by the *U.S.S. Brooklyn*.[34] Farragut later turned the vessel over to General Butler whose troops were in the process of occupying the forts and strategic points along the river in the general New Orleans area.

While disposing of the *Diana*, Farragut wrote Butler that the owner of the steamer claimed to be a good Union man and wanted his boat back. But the flag officer doubted this claim and stipulated that the vessel was a lawful prize and subject to seizure by the United States.[35]

According to a *New York Times* newspaper article, the *Diana* was listed as a river boat which was loaded with "loafers, gentlemen, and others who came down from New Orleans to witness the fight" at the forts. It was stated further that the boat escaped up river, but was subsequently captured.[36]

The *Diana*, however, was privately owned by the Houston Navigation Co. and apparently chartered to the Confederate government where it was utilized for the transfer of troops, supplies, sundries, and miscellaneous items along the lower Gulf Coast including New Orleans and

159

ENROLLMENT.

ENROLLMENT.

In conformity to an Act of the Congress of the **UNITED STATES OF AMERICA**, entitled "An Act for the enrolling and licensing **SHIPS OR VESSELS**, to be employed in the **COASTING TRADE AND FISHERIES**, and for regulating the same."

John H. Sterrett of Houston Texas
having taken or subscribed the Oath required by the said Act, and having sworn that he owns 1/3
B. A. Shepherd 1/3 and S. W. Smith 1/3 all of same place

are _____ citizens of the UNITED STATES,

No. 159

Temporary

WHERE SURRENDERED

District of New Orleans
Galveston

DATE OF SURRENDER.

21 day of June 1860

CAUSE OF SURRENDER.

J. C. ir

James A. Gibson
Surveyor, &c.,

the owners of the Ship or Vessel called the Diana of Pittsburgh whereof John H. Sterrett is at present Master, and as he hath sworn is a citizen of the UNITED STATES, and that the said Ship or Vessel was built at Brownsville Pa in the year 1858, as appears by her Certificate of Admeasurement No. 51 dated and issued at Pittsburgh November 3d 1858 and having filed certificate of Hull & Boiler Inspection according to act of Congress of August 30 1852. And the Deputy Surveyor of the Port of Pittsburgh having certified that the said Ship or Vessel has one deck and no mast and that her length is 165 feet ___ in. her breadth 26 4 her depth 5 9 and that she measures two hundred & thirty Nine as 7/95 to 239 7/95 tons, and that she is a Steamer has Transom Stern Cabin on deck and no ___ head And the said John H. Sterrett having agreed to the description and admeasurement above specified, and sufficient security having been given according to the said Act, the said Steam Boat Diana has been duly enrolled at the Port of Pittsburgh.

GIVEN Under my Hand and Seal at the
PORT OF PITTSBURGH,
this 3d day of November in the year one thousand eight hundred and fifty Eight

Enrollment certificate of the steamer *Diana*, given on November 3rd, 1858 at the Port of Pittsburgh. The steamer was later converted into a gunboat by Union General Benjamin Butler. (National Archives, Washington, D.C.)

Port Hudson. One report claimed that its master was M.N. Radovich.[37]

The *Diana* was built in Brownsville, Pennsylvania in 1858 and described as a stout little sidewheel steamer with a cabin above deck, a transom stern, and a plain head. She was a 239 tonner, 165 feet long, 26 feet 4 inches wide, and 5 feet 9 inches deep. She was enrolled at the Port of Galveston on the 21st of December, 1858 and owned by three men, B.A. Shepherd, F.W. Smith, and John H. Sterrett—all of Houston, Texas. The vessel was originally involved in coastal trade and fisheries.[38]

General Butler assumed command of the city of New Orleans on May 1, 1862 and took advantage of the *Diana*, putting her to good use as an army transport on the Mississippi and Red Rivers.[39]

The Battle of Baton Rouge which was fought in August, 1862. (*Harper's Weekly*)

Chapter 2

YANKEE PENETRATION

FOLLOWING THE FALL OF NEW ORLEANS, LOUISI-ana, Governor Thomas O. Moore ordered the state capital moved from Baton Rouge to Opelousas and wrote Confederate President Jefferson Davis that the Confederate forces in Louisiana were disorganized and that the situation was causing unrest and internal dissension.[1] After the Federal forces occupied Baton Rouge on May 28, 1862, the Confederacy formed a new department called the Trans-Mississippi which included the State of Louisiana. Governor Moore soon began the organization of troops for the defense of the state and built training camps at Opelousas, Monroe, and New Iberia.[2]

Texas Partisan Rangers, who were stationed near the Mississippi River town of Donaldsonville, Louisiana, fired upon Federal transports and other vessels which passed along the river.[3] The Federals threatened to shell the town if the sniper action continued. The firing did continue and Farragut became enraged. He ordered the evacuation of men, women, and children from Donaldsonville and three days later sent several of his gunboats to shell the city. A detachment went ashore with torches and destroyed most of the business section of town, a number of houses, and some plantations along the river. Farragut warned that he would repeat the action every time his boats were fired upon.[4]

When the Bayou Country dwellers of Louisiana learned that Yankees had gained a foothold on Louisiana soil, they became terrified. They'd heard that the invaders had plundered homes, smashed furniture, and looted precious articles. Since the main Confederate troops were stationed on other fronts, the citizens found themselves unprotected and vulnerable to attacks by the enemy.[5]

Governor Moore, cognizant of the perilous situation, pleaded to Jefferson Davis for help. The President sent General Richard Taylor to command the Confederate forces in the District of Western Louisiana. On July 28, 1862, Taylor was detached from the Second Louisiana Brigade and promoted to the rank of major general. After reaching Opelousas, he met with Governor Moore who turned the small bodies of troops and campsites he had halfway organized over to Taylor, and the general immediately took charge, making Alexandria his district headquarters.[6]

General Taylor was prominent in many respects. He was the son of President Zachary Taylor, a member of the Louisiana Legislature, the owner of a sugar plantation in St. Charles Parish, a hero in the Virginia campaign, and the former brother-in-law of President Davis. (His sister, Sarah Knox Taylor, was Davis' first wife.)

Taylor was well-informed in the art of battle having received "on the scene" coaching from the master himself, his father, during the Mexican campaign. Dick Taylor's ex-

Confederate General Richard Taylor.

Confederate General Alfred Mouton.

perience in the Virginia arena of warfare, coupled with his knowledge of Louisiana swamps and bayous, made him an ideal choice for the new post.

He lost no time in carrying out his responsibility. He indicated that he had found one camp of instruction established at Monroe but was disappointed that few conscripts had enrolled there. He then established a camp of instruction at Camp Pratt which was located on Lake Tasse near the Nickerson Pecan Grove and about six miles northwest of New Iberia. This camp was named after John G. Pratt of the Parish of Saint Landry who was a brigadier general in the state militia.[7]

Taylor placed Lt. Colonel R.E. Burke of the Second Louisiana Regiment in command at Camp Pratt and consequently succeeded in enrolling about 3,000 persons as conscripts. Of this number, nearly 2,000 were ordered to his district and the remainder sent to Louisiana troops serving at or near Port Hudson. Later, Lt. Colonel Burke was replaced by Colonel Eugene Waggaman and returned to his regiment in Virginia.[8]

In the meantime, the citizens of Louisiana, especially New Orleanians, had acquired an intense hatred for General Butler. Because of his reported uncouth and inhumane actions, he was labeled "The Beast." They claimed that William B. Mumford, a citizen of New Orleans, was executed for pulling down a U.S. flag before the city had formally surrendered. They also remembered the infamous "General Order No. 28" issued May 15, 1862, that read in part:

> Hereafter, when any female shall, by word, gesture, or movement, insult or show con-

tempt for any officer or soldier of the United
States, she shall be regarded and held liable
to be treated as a woman of the town plying
her avocation.[9]

There were charges that peaceful and aged citizens were
confined at hard labor with ball and chain and that helpless
women were torn from their homes and subjected to solitary
confinement. Also, it was reported that sugar planters were
threatened with having slaves driven from the plantations
unless the owners consented to share the crops with General
Butler, and other Union officers.[10]

There were accusations that the entire population of New
Orleans was forced to choose between starvation by the confiscation of all their property or taking an oath against con-
science to bear allegiance to the invaders of the country. There
were reports that slaves had been incited to insurrection and
armed for a servile war—"a war in its nature far exceeding in
horrors the most merciless atrocities of the savages."[11]

Butler even received criticism from his own officers. Lt.
F.A. Roe, commander of the U.S. gunboat *Katahdin,* while
escorting three transports to Donaldsonville on September
11th, stated in a report to Commodore Henry Morris that the
activities of Federal troops were both "disgraceful and
humiliating."

He reported that troops had entered a large mansion,
pillaged it in a brutal manner and carried off wines, liquors,
silver, and clothing belonging to the women. He added that
the soldiers were intoxicated, undisciplined, and licentious.
Lt. Roe asked to be relieved of service requiring him to guard
troops engaged in such disgraceful acts.[12]

Colonel Edwin Waller. (Sketch by the author)

In the meantime, some of Butler's troops, who were active along the west bank of the Mississippi, penetrated into the LaFourche area where they established a military post at Bayou Des Allemands. This caused more unrest and concern for the Confederate command, but Taylor was ready for action. He sent Colonel Edwin Waller, Jr., with his cavalry of Texas riflemen, along with a contingent of General Pratt's state militia to attack the post.

The invading Confederate force played havoc at Des Allemands and Boutte, capturing two companies of infantry including guns and ammunition, burning a railroad station, and setting fire to transports and bridges. Louisiana rejoiced at this victory, small though it was.[13]

But Colonel Waller and his 13th Texas Cavalry, which was made up of rugged veterans of the Mexican war, foreigners, and bold Texans, were dead set on pursuing more Yankees. He directed his next attack along the river road towards St. Charles Parish. Taylor, whose home was located in this vicinity, warned Waller to be careful while deploying troops there because they could be easily trapped. However, Waller, having immunity of attack for several days, became careless.[14]

Butler, who was infuriated by the marauding attacks on his military units and shipping, set out to get Waller whose forces were spotted on the west bank of the Mississippi River in the vicinity of the St. Charles Parish Courthouse. The Union general immediately ordered Colonel James McMillan to take a portion of the 21st Indiana Regiment and 9th Connecticut and land below Waller's forces. He also sent Colonel Halbert Paine with the 14th Maine and 4th Wisconsin to land above Waller. They used transports in the deployment of troops accompanied by the armed steamer *Mississippi*.[15]

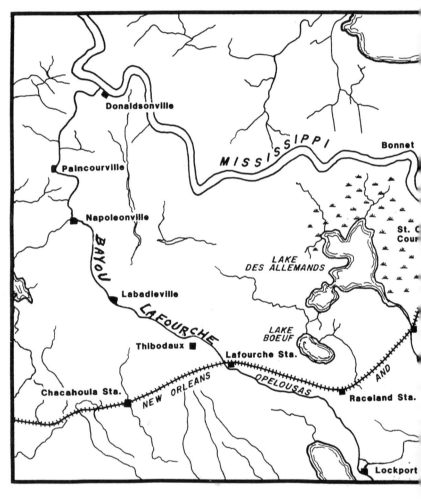

Map of Southeast Louisiana showing the New Orleans area, the LaFourche

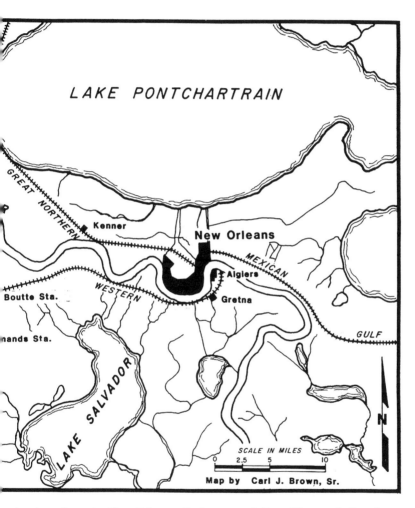

LAKE PONTCHARTRAIN

GREAT NORTHERN

Kenner

New Orleans

MEXICAN

Algiers

Boutte Sta.

WESTERN

Gretna

nands Sta.

GULF

LAKE SALVADOR

N

SCALE IN MILES

0   2.5   5   10

Map by   Carl J. Brown, Sr.

and points along the New Orleans, Opelousas, and Great Western Railroad.

A Gunboat Named Diana

This maneuver was successfully executed, entrapping the entire Confederate force at a point approximately three miles above the St. Charles Courthouse. Waller, who found his battalion hemmed in between the Mississippi River and a treacherous swamp, refused to surrender and ordered his troops to hide in a sugar cane field. They were unmounted and every fourth man held horses, but an accidental shot exposed their location and immediately they became the targets of a heated barrage of gunfire.[16]

According to C.C. Cox, who was acting as adjutant for Waller at the time, the Confederates were caught in the crossfire from above and below and "the gunboat sent shot and shell faster and faster." The group stood fast. Waller then gave the order to break ranks saying, "Get to your horses and fall back into the woods." This caused a regular stampede for the swamp.

After penetrating about 200 yards through deep water, soft mud, and cypress knees, the troops experienced difficulty in advancing their horses any further. Much to their sorrow, the men were forced to abandon their horses, saddles, and accouterments. After bogging through the swamp most of the day, the tired and hungry remnants of Waller's battalion finally made it to "Dick" Taylor's plantation by nightfall.[17]

This was a tragic defeat for Waller. Colonel McMillan's report revealed that the Union forces captured 50 prisoners, 300 horses and saddles, two Rebel flags, one French flag, shotguns, and pistols. He also indicated that there were several of the enemy dead and wounded. Waller's men then skirted the woods that same night, backtracking toward their base. They reached the railroad station at Boutte by daylight

52

and began walking the railroad track toward Bayou Des Allemands where the state militia was located.

From the day the Texans first rode into South Louisiana with their beautiful horses, fancy saddles and cocky stride, a sort of ribbing had erupted that was to last for the duration of the campaign. The Cajuns at times would razz the Texans, and the Texans were sure to direct their periodic verbal flings at the Cajuns. But when the chips were down, both factions teamed up in the finest fashion and fought side by side in mutual respect and admiration.

Waller's cavalrymen, who were extremely weary, became embarrassed as they approached the camp on foot. Cox wrote, "This left our little band of heroic Texians (sic) in a bad plight and our humiliation and discomfiture in the presence of the victorious Kageans (sic) was most mortifying. Now we are on foot, dismounted, and degraded to the infantry service."

Colonel Waller was very unhappy with the condition of his command and planned to do something about it. He succeeded in getting an interview with General Taylor, who was at his headquarters in Alexandria. The colonel made an ardent plea to have his battalion remounted and suggested, furthermore, that he, Waller, could detail an officer from each of his companies to return to Texas and secure the necessary number of horses. Taylor agreed to the request, much to Waller's delight.

On October 17, 1862, Waller's units received a dispatch ordering them to Lake Charles on the Calcasieu River, with the assurance that the men would be remounted. This news was received with immense joy for Waller's cavalry had borne the embarrassment of being without horses since the September 8th retreat through the swamps.[18]

A Gunboat Named Diana

Around the 1st of October, Confederate Colonel Alfred Mouton, who had recovered from an injury received during the battle of Shiloh, was promoted to brigadier general and reported to General Taylor for duty. General Mouton, a West Pointer and native of Vermilionville (Lafayette), Louisiana, was revered for his courage and patriotism. He was delighted with his assignment to the LaFourche District where he was reunited with the Acadians of the 18th Louisiana Regiment. Mouton, headquartered at Thibodaux with a force of approximately 1,400 men, was to picket the Des Allemands-Donaldsonville area.[19]

General Butler made plans for an all-out invasion of South Louisiana which included the immediate dislodging of Mouton from his threatening position. Butler began organizing an expedition consisting of five regiments, two batteries of artillery, and four companies of cavalry, all under the command of his military adviser, Godfrey Weitzel, who had been promoted to the rank of brigadier general. This brigade was to move upon the western bank of the Mississippi and then continue southwardly through the LaFourche country.

At the same time, Butler would deploy the 8th Regiment Vermont Volunteers, and the 1st Regiment of Native Guards along the Opelousas Railroad which stretched from Algiers (near New Orleans) to Brashear City (Morgan City). He stated that by gaining control of the railroad he would assist Weitzel in the way of supplies, and "give loyal planters an opportunity to forward their sugar and cotton to this city" (meaning New Orleans).[20]

Butler also proposed to send some light-draft steamers which he had been outfitting for service for deployment in shallow bayous and lakes. He protected their boilers and engines with iron coverings "so as to prevent, if possible, the recurrence of the dreadful accident which occurred in the Mound City steamer by the penetration of her boilers." Light guns were to be mounted on the steamers and they were to attack batteries at Berwick Bay, penetrate the waters of the bay and tributaries, cut off the supplies of cattle which were destined for the Rebel army, and assist the Union troops in dispersing and capturing Taylor's forces. [21]

One of these vessels which was outfitted for this daring invasion was the gunboat *Diana*. This vessel was equipped with fine armament. There were five guns mounted on her bow which consisted of one 30-pounder Parrott rifle pivot, two smooth bore 32-pounders, and two 12-pounder bronze Dahlgren rifled boat howitzers. The *Diana* was well-protected, casemated forward and on the sides around the boilers and engines, but had no protection aft. The casemate consisted of two thicknesses of 4″ x 1¼″ bars of wrought iron laid flat on wood backing built at an angle of thirty to forty degrees. [22]

(In Mrs. Routh Trowbridge Wilby's recent book, *Clearing Bayou Teche after the Civil War—The Kingsbury Project,* it was reported on April 24, 1871, by the foreman Daniel Kingsbury that 23 plates of wrought iron 7″ x 1″ were removed from the remains of the *Diana*. Twelve of these plates were 12′x9″ inches long. These plates may have been added later on during the Teche campaign as extra protection to the engines and boilers.) [23]

Other shallow draft gunboats which were equipped for the Bayou Country assignment were the *Estrella, Calhoun,* and the *Kinsman*. The Navy was to furnish the officers and crew. [24]

Union General Godfrey Weitzel.

Confederate General H.H. Sibley.

Chapter 3

CAPTURE OF BERWICK BAY

GENERAL WEITZEL, WHO WAS ORGANIZED AND ready to proceed with the LaFourche campaign, had his troops board transports. On the 24th of October, 1862, his flotilla, under the protective convoy of the gunboats *Kineo, Scoita, Katahdin,* and *Itasca,* steamed up the Mississippi from the New Orleans area for about a hundred miles and landed just below Donaldsonville.[1]

The Weitzel brigade numbered around 4,000. It included the 75th New York; 8th New Hampshire; 12th and 13th Connecticut; 1st Louisiana Infantry; Troop C of the Massachusetts Cavalry; Williamson's, Barret's, and Carruth's Louisiana Cavalry; and Thompson's Batteries.[2]

Captain John De Forest of the 12th Connecticut stated that the troops landed the following day at "the once flourishing little town of Donaldsonville—a desert of smoke-blackened ruins." He added that his regiment slept on the floor of a Catholic church, and that he ate his supper off of a tombstone in the cemetery.[3]

On Sunday, October 26, the Union forces began their march down the banks of Bayou LaFourche along with a floating bridge which they utilized in crossing soldiers as they advanced.

In the meantime, General Mouton with around 1,400 men moved up the bayou deploying his units on both banks. They were: the 18th, 33rd, Crescent, and Terrebonne regiments; Ralston's and Semmes' batteries; the 2nd Louisiana Cavalry, and a cavalry detachment. Though inferior in numbers, the Confederates resisted the Union thrust at a settlement called Texas in Assumption Parish, effectively checking its advance—but the Rebels eventually gave way, falling back about a mile and a half to Labadieville where they intended to make a stand.[4]

Mouton, having been informed that the Union Command had plans to make simultaneous movements via Donaldsonville, Des Allemands, and Berwick Bay, became greatly concerned that his forces were vulnerable to being trapped. He contacted his quartermaster to provide a train to evacuate Colonel T.E. Vick's troops out of the Des Allemands-Boutte area, and the St. Charles and St. John the Baptist regiments and cavalry pickets. He instructed the colonel to save everything he could, destroy everything he might be compelled to leave behind, and fall back without delay to join the main body.[5]

Colonel Vick and his men, however, could not utilize the train because of a mix-up requiring a written order. He did make the most of his withdrawal, destroying the depot and bridge at Des Allemands, but the tedious march along the railroad bed was painful. When Vick's forces reached Mouton at 3 p.m. on the 28th, they were tired, worn out, and arrived later than was expected, causing more problems for Mouton.[6]

According to De Forest, the Union troops advanced "like greenhorns, straggling about the road, the levee, the fields, and taking advantage of every discoverable cut-off." They passed "pretty houses, flourishing plantations, and endless flats of waving cane." He mentioned that "a tall, cadaverous man with lank iron-grey hair, and the voice of a camp-meeting preacher, shouted lugubrious warnings to us. 'Ah boys! boys! you don't know what awaits you. You are going to defeat, and rout, and slaughter. Better turn back while you can! Better turn back!' Some of the youngsters yelled impertinences to him, and he stalked solemnly into his house, leaving our impenitent array to its fate."[7]

On the 27th of October, a spirited engagement erupted on the Labadieville front at Georgia Landing. Mouton, lacking reinforcements, maneuvered with his enemy and resisted as best he could. He issued orders for the removal of the sick to Berwick Bay and made all needful preparations for the removal of stores.

On the following day, he withdrew slowly while holding the Yankees at bay. He realized that the door was now open for a Union thrust by way of Des Allemands and Boutte. He was also informed that two transports and two gunboats were landing reinforcements at the Assumption cut-off, and there were rumors afloat that the Union expedition by way of the Gulf of Mexico to Berwick Bay had reached its destination. He decided to fall back to Terre Bonne station, evacuate all the stores and troops by train, and then move to Berwick Bay as quickly as possible.[8]

Mouton reported his casualties in the engagement at Georgia Landing as five killed, eight wounded, and 186 missing. He painfully regretted the death of Colonel G.P.

59

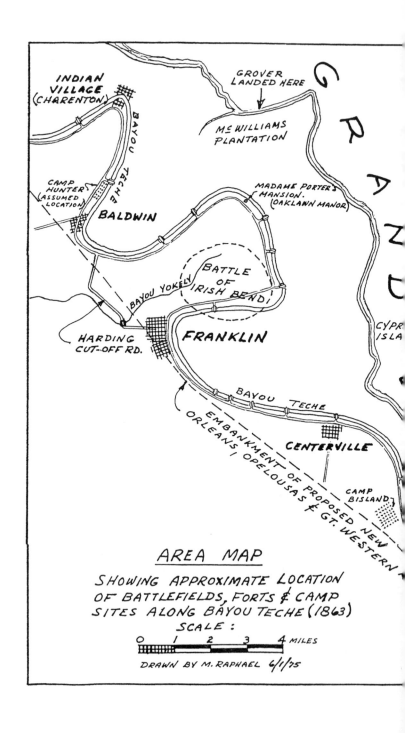

INDIAN VILLAGE (CHARENTON)

GROVER LANDED HERE

G R A N D

McWILLIAMS PLANTATION

BAYOU TECHE

CAMP HUNTER (ASSUMED LOCATION)

BALDWIN

MADAME PORTER'S MANSION. (OAKLAWN MANOR)

BATTLE OF IRISH BEND

BAYOU YOKELY

FRANKLIN

CYPR ISLA

HARDING CUT-OFF RD.

BAYOU TECHE

EMBANKMENT OF PROPOSED NEW ORLEANS, OPELOUSAS & GT. WESTERN

CENTERVILLE

CAMP BISLAND

AREA MAP

SHOWING APPROXIMATE LOCATION OF BATTLEFIELDS, FORTS & CAMP SITES ALONG BAYOU TECHE (1863)

SCALE:

0   1   2   3   4 MILES

DRAWN BY M. RAPHAEL 6/1/75

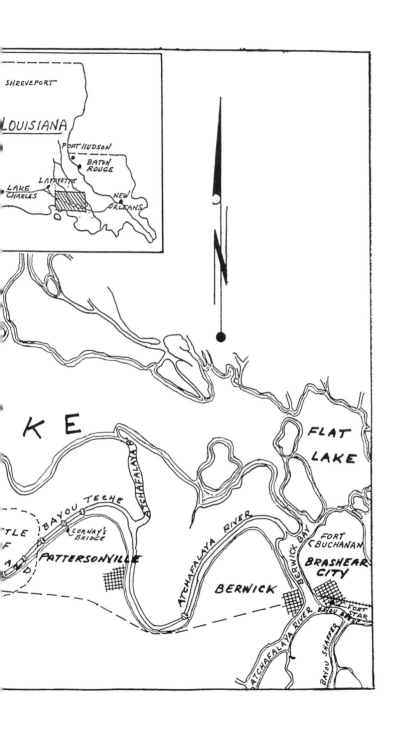

McPheeters of the Crescent Regiment, and Captain George Ralston who commanded the battery. According to Weitzel, the Union losses were 18 killed, 74 wounded, and five missing. Captains John Warren and John Kelleher of the 8th New Hampshire were killed.

By 4 p.m. October 28, Mouton had collected nearly all of his troops. He set fire to the LaFourche Crossing Bridge and the Terre Bonne Railroad Station, then moved on with his cavalry, reaching Brashear City on the 29th. The bridge at Bayou Boeuf was also burned. On the following day, Mouton found himself in a fortunate position as he managed to transfer everything safely across Berwick Bay, and maintain his command of the forces and vessels in that vicinity.[9]

Weitzel, however, claimed that his cavalry was in close pursuit of the Rebels and prevented the total destruction of the Bayou LaFourche and Bayou Terre Bonne bridges.[10]

General Butler had named Lieutenant Commander Thomas McKean Buchanan to lead the flotilla of "beefed-up," shallow-draft gunboats and transport in an effort to cut off Mouton's retreat and capture Berwick Bay.[11] Buchanan left Lake Pontchartrain on the afternoon of October 25th aboard his flagship, the *Calhoun,* and proceeded to Southwest Pass where he met the gunboat *Estrella,* and the transport *St. Mary's.* The gunboat *Kinsman,* which had broken down at Fort Pike, and the gunboat *Diana*, which did not have its complement of officers and crew, were left behind to follow as soon as possible. The *Diana* began taking on volunteers from the frigate *Mississippi,* and Edmund C. Weeks was placed in command as Acting Master. Captain George W. Kendall was actually the official commander of the vessel, but he allowed Weeks to take charge because, as he stated: "I was entirely ignorant of the science of navigation, and Mr. Weeks being with me, enabled me to find my way with the assistance of charts." Alfred Pierson, also on board, and Weeks had been Kendall's mates aboard the U.S. transport *Ceres,* which burned off Ship Island on October 7, 1862.

In the meantime, Buchanan had the 21st Indiana Infantry Regiment board the *St. Mary's,* and his small fleet set out along the coast headed for its destination. Buchanan arrived at the Atchafalaya Bay on the morning of the 29th of October with two gunboats, a transport, and a coal schooner, but was deeply troubled to learn that the Rebels had removed the buoys and stakes that marked the intricate and narrow channel which led to the Atchafalaya River. Adding to his miseries was a low tide caused by a stiff north wind, and there were also obstructions that loomed ahead.[12]

In the evening, after working their way to the obstructions, the *Kinsman* arrived. Its pilot found himself busy all night long putting down stakes so that the vessels would steer clear of the obstructions. Buchanan encountered even more problems—the *Calhoun* and *Estrella* could hardly navigate, going aground several times. He then transferred guns and ammunition from his vessel to the *Kinsman* as they waited for a high tide to get afloat.

Taking advantage of the invaders' predicament, a Rebel steamer, the *Hart,* attacked, firing three guns at the bogged-down fleet. Buchanan stated that after he returned "two guns" from his 30-pound Parrott, the steamer "turned and ran back."[13]

Buchanan finally made it to Berwick Bay by the evening of November 1—48 hours too late in cutting off Mouton's

The Confederate gunboat *Cotton* and its courageous crew led by Captain
E. W. Fuller fought off four Union gunboats. (*Frank Leslie's Illustrated
Newspaper,* Feb. 21, 1863)

retreat. The Rebel gunboat *Cotton,* under the command of
E.W. Fuller, made its appearance in the bay, and Buchanan,
who was aboard the *Kinsman,* gave chase but stated that
"she got away from us by her superior speed." The Union
fleet commander however succeeded in capturing a small
steamer, the *A.B. Seger,* which he reported would be very
useful in his operations.[14]

Fuller's account revealed that the *Seger,* under command
of I.C. Coons, disobeyed Mouton's order to proceed up the
lake. Instead he turned up the Atchafalaya and was "ignobly
abandoned to the enemy at a time when the *Cotton* was between the enemy and the *Seger.*" Fuller stated further that
Coons abandoned his men and boat and proceeded as fast as
possible to St. Martinville."[15]

According to General Taylor, Captain Edward W. Fuller
was a western steamboat man and one of the "bravest of a
bold daring class."Fuller was a former state representative
from St. Martin Parish, Louisiana. Shortly after the fall of
New Orleans, he received a commission from Governor
Thomas Moore to raise a company of volunteers which was
called the St. Martin Rangers, and later called "Fuller's
Company Bull Battery." He was placed in charge of convert-
ing the large river steamboat, the *Cotton,* into a gunboat,
which he did successfully with the aid of Major J.L. Brent.[16]

The *Cotton* was called "The Terror of the Teche" and
was named after John L. Cotton, an ardent Union man and
wealthy planter of Louisiana who "opposed secession to the
last." But, after the state legislature passed the ordinance of
seccession, "he espoused the Confederate cause with equal
enthusiasm and fitted out his steamer and presented it to the
Confederacy."[17]

A Gunboat Named Diana

The *Cotton* was actually the only heavily armed gunboat under General Mouton's command. The vessel was armed with one 32- and two 24-pounders (smooth bore) located on her bow, and one 9-pounder (rifle bore) on her deck. The 9-pounder was cast from plantation bells and named *St. Mary* after the parish in which the gunboat was operating. Other craft available to the Confederate general were the *Hart* and several light sloops. The *Hart,* an iron-clad steamer, which had been transporting stores, ordnance, and troops in support of the Rebels in the Berwick Bay area, was in the process of towing a sugar barge up Bayou Teche. Although she came to the assistance of the *Cotton,* she was ordered to resume her towing assignment.[18]

Buchanan, who was aboard the *Kinsman* and along with the *Estrella* in Berwick Bay awaiting his other vessels, was suddenly attacked by the *Cotton* with Fuller at the helm. Buchanan gave chase, but was upset and puzzled that one of his guns was spiked (an iron piece driven into the barrel). He ordered the *Estrella* to open fire with her guns, and the *Cotton* retaliated with one of its guns striking the *Kinsman* under the port bow. Fuller however, careful not to expose his vessel too freely in a situation where he was overpowered, backed out of action and steamed up the Atchafalya River. The transport, *St. Mary's,* arrived to join Buchanan's fleet as they anchored off Brashear City for the night.[19]

On the following day, November 2nd, Buchanan was relieved that the *Diana* and *Calhoun* finally made it to Berwick Bay. His fleet was now intact and ready for action. They landed at Brashear City, which was actually a small town of about 300 people. The place was strategic in many respects: It was the terminus of a railroad which linked south central Louisiana to the New Orleans area; a port of entry that contained a deep harbor, wharves, and storehouses; and stood out as an important reconnoitering point for water traffic that operated to and from the gulf, bays, rivers, bayous, and lakes in that vast, low-lying region of the country.[20]

Brashear City was described as a "miserable dirty village of a dozen houses" where six years earlier there had been nothing but a few Indian mounds and cane fields. But there was also a hotel, coffee shop, dry goods store, a bar, and a few other business establishments alongside the tracks. Another scribe stated that the town consisted of a few houses, a dilapidated wharf, and lots of mud. A Louisiana contraband remarked that the town had been "borned and hadn't growed." (Escaped slaves supported by the Federal government were called "contrabands.")[21]

General Weitzel, who had been based at Thibodaux, deployed his troops as far as Berwick Bay, and at the same time ordered Colonel Stephen Thomas of the 8th Vermont Volunteers to make necessary repairs and replacements along the 80-mile stretch of the New Orleans and Opelousas Railroad which extended from Algiers to Brashear City. This work for Thomas included rebuilding the railroad bridges at LaFourche Crossing and Bayou Boeuf, rebuilding culverts, repairing railroad tracks, and even clearing the tracks of weeds and debris.[22]

As the Federal troops expanded their occupation of LaFourche and St. Mary parishes, many Negro slaves from the various plantations began to desert their masters and joined the victory train. At Brashear City, over four hundred wagonloads of Negroes were left behind by the Confederates in their hasty retreat. Weitzel complained that he had twice as many Negroes around his camp at Thibodaux as he had soldiers and he didn't know what to do with them. He couldn't feed them and, as a consequence, they had to find food for themselves. He reported that many of the white citizens of the community, who had already taken an oath of allegiance, begged to retain their arms for fear of attack from belligerent Negroes. Although a new district was being set up with Weitzel in command, the general expressed his hesitancy to accept under the prevailing circumstances.[23]

Union Major George Strong, who was the assistant adjutant general, explained to Weitzel that by an act of Congress those Negroes who left their masters in occupied territory were free. He emphasized that it was the duty of the Federal command to take care of them, and one way of doing it was by employment. He suggested sending the Negroes back to the plantations to help on the sugar crops for those owners who were loyal and work for the United States where the owners were disloyal. Weitzel, however, was quick to respond to Strong citing several instances where the plantation plan didn't work.[24]

The arrival of Colonel James McMillan and his 21st Indiana Infantry aboard the troop ship *St. Mary's* was a relief to Weitzel in that there were mechanics, locomotive builders, and bridge constructors. Although Buchanan failed to cut off Mouton, his capture of Berwick Bay sealed off the Confederates from that point eastward as far as the Mississippi River area.[25]

Chapter 4

THE STRIFE AT CORNAY'S BRIDGE

AS SOON AS MOUTON CROSSED OVER TO THE
west side of Berwick Bay, he made immediate arrangements
to block the Union forces from penetrating into the Teche
country. He assigned Colonel Valery Sulakowski, who was
chief engineer with the Corps of Engineers, to select a temporary position about a half mile upstream of the mouth of
Bayou Teche in the vicinity of the Charpentier place. Further
upstream in the Teche, obstructions were placed at Cornay's
bridge. This consisted of the steamer *Flycatcher* and a
schooner loaded with bricks—both were sunk crossways in
the channel. Live oaks were also thrown in to make the barrier even more difficult to penetrate.[1]

Then, about two miles further upstream at Mrs. Meade's
in the vicinity of the Bisland estate, Mouton gathered a
Negro labor force which he used in the construction of a
rather strong fortification with entrenchments and heavy
guns erected on both sides of the bayou. This stronghold
became known as Fort Bisland named after the donor of a
large tract of land for the Confederate cause.[2]

The Meade site was carefully selected by Taylor and Mouton in that the position represented a line of embankment stretched across a narrow neck of the Teche ridge with Grand Lake on the north and a reach of Vermilion Bay swamp on the south. The bayou, however, at this point was open and the railroad embankment to the south served as additional protection for the Confederate land forces. Taylor conveyed his theory to Mouton that field pieces in close quarters against gunboats would be advantageous in bayou warfare. [3]

On November 3rd, 1862, Buchanan coaled up his fleet of four gunboats, the *Diana, Calhoun, Estrella,* and the *Kinsman,* and steamed up the Atchafalaya in pursuit of the *Cotton.* He found Mouton's temporary fortification deserted and reported that the Rebels had retreated to Cornay's bridge where they were posted for battle.

Fuller had been ordered by Mouton to delay the Union fleet as much as possible in order to provide time for construction of the fortifications at Bisland. Fuller and Buchanan blasted away at each other. But from the start, the Union Lt. Commander had problems. His Parrott gun was somewhat fouled up and needed repair. He sent two boats ahead which were met by heavy gunfire from the *Cotton,* striking the *Estrella* on the port rail, killing two soldiers who were operating the 24-pounder howitzer, and wounding another. [4]

The *Estrella's* wheel ropes were also carried away in the exchange and, since the bayou was so narrow, she managed to pull ashore to allow the other boats to pass. The *Diana* and *Kinsman* then got into action when again, the Union attackers encountered trouble. The *Diana,* which had Parrott

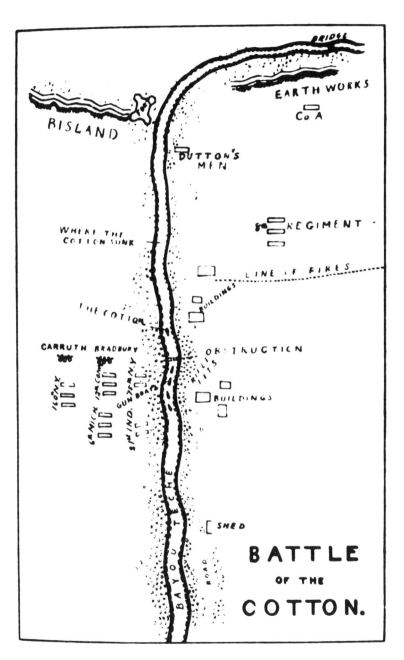

From Carpenter's *History of the 8th Vermont*.

guns mounted on an iron carriage, also got fouled up and she too moved out of action.[5]

The *Colonel Kinsman,* like the *Diana*, was captured in New Orleans by Farragut's fleet and was also fitted out by Butler to be used in the bayou campaign. The boilers and machinery of the *Kinsman* were protected by iron and the vessel was under the command of Acting Master George Wiggins. He courageously maneuvered his vessel up to the bridge where his crew was showered with gunfire from all directions. Wiggins succeeded in fighting off eleven fieldpieces and blasted away at the *Cotton* with his rifled gun. The *Cotton* however was about 1,000 yards upstream of Cornay's bridge and the obstructions, pouring shot and shell at the *Kinsman.*[6]

The following are interesting excerpts from the diary of George Baird, assistant engineer on the *Calhoun,* concerning the day's activities:

> The *Diana* went up the Atchafalaya River toward Pattersonville and found the *Cotton* was in the Teche, and returned; then all four vessels went up the river and into the Teche up to Cornay's bridge, where the obstructions were. Saw a steam mud excavator on fire up the bayou.
>
> The *J.A. Cotton* opened up on us at 1:30 p.m. and we replied. She struck the *Calhoun* eight times. One shot carried our soup tureen and our roast beef into the paddle wheel, another struck the shaft, and one went through and through the hull at low-water line. Two of our men were killed and some wounded. A splinter cut my left hand

and brought blood. The land batteries put 54 shot through the upper works of the *Kinsman*. It was beautiful to see Buchanan sight the pivot gun; he landed a percussion shell on the *Cotton's* armor which exploded and cleared her deck. Two or three such shot served to drive the *Cotton* up the bayou. Our bell wires were shot away; they were repaired during the action. The breeching of a 32-pounder was shot away, the paint locker destroyed. The land batteries did most of the firing on the *Kinsman*, but when Buchanan sighted a 32-pounder with cannister at them they limbered up their guns and left like men in a hurry.[7]

According to Fuller's report, the four Federal gunboats mounted 27 guns which "gave us broadside after broadside, frequently the four delivering their fire at once." He added that several of the Union boats were hit hard and fell out of action, and when "victory seemed to be within our reach, it was announced that we had no more cartridges, having fired the last one."

While backing slowly upstream, Fuller had sacks made by "cutting off the legs from the pantaloons of some of the men which we filled and returned fire with as often as we could . . . This we continued until we were out of range and the enemy ceased their fire." Fuller reported that they lost one soldier who was killed accidentally—three others were wounded, one of whom died later.[8]

Buchanan stated that the *Cotton's* firing was excellent. The *Calhoun* received eight shots (as already mentioned by Baird) and that none did any material damage. The *Estrella*

The Gunboat Battle at Cornay's Bridge (From *Harper's Weekly*.)

and *Diana* were each hit three times with no damage to the machinery, but the *Kinsman*, which had one killed and five wounded, was moved out of action.

Later, when the *Cotton* withdrew upstream and out of range, the *Diana* and *Estrella* rejoined the *Calhoun*. The three vessels shelled the woods, drove off the land forces, and landed near the bridge. They tried to remove the obstructions and also tried to force the *Diana* through the heap, but were unsuccessful in both attempts. This was definitely not a good day for Buchanan. Besides suffering casualties, the *Kinsman* was riddled and leaking badly, and the *Diana* was eventually hauled out because her stern was shot away.

A few days later, Buchanan, on board the *Calhoun*, ventured to the vicinity of Cornay's bridge along with the *Estrella*, leaving his other two boats at Brashear City to be repaired. He wasn't so lucky on this occasion either as a shot from the *Cotton* struck his port forward Parrott gun, killing two crewmen instantly. He claimed, however, that he drove the Rebels off.

Fuller reported that the Union gunboats came in sight firing from a point out of range and that he returned fire so accurately that the vessels left after a 55 minute contest. He stated further that the two gunboats were badly damaged, and "their loss heavy—ours nothing . . . this victory was clearly ours. The enemy retired from action badly discouraged with severe loss. We were unhurt." Although the Union vessels approached again on the following day and fired, they didn't come within sight of the *Cotton* which was poised near the bridge.[9]

Buchanan was pestered with Rebel field artillery units

which were posted on both banks and, in a communication to Butler, stated that there was nothing he could do until Weitzel arrived with his troops. "They are strongly posted at the obstructions," he wrote, "and although I can drive them off, I cannot work at them. We want some more ammunition now, badly. I think the *Cotton* is casemated, as our shell glanced off. We had him on fire once. We could plainly see our shot strike him, but he fights bows on." Buchanan mentioned that the Rebel force there numbered between 3,000 and 4,000 men with 70 field pieces. But according to Taylor, Mouton had only about 10 guns and 1,300 men during this period. There was also a floating bridge which was used further upstream to accommodate troops in bayou crossing.[10]

General Taylor was so elated with Fuller's courageous performances that he recommended to Judah Benjamin, secretary of state, that the captain of the *Cotton* be bestowed some mark of favor for his singlehanded gallantry in defeating four gunboats. Benjamin in turn suggested to Secretary of War James Seddon that perhaps a promotion would be just reward for Fuller's outstanding services. Adjutant General Samuel Cooper, however, wrote that the only thing that could be done at that time was to write a letter of commendation, and that if a vacancy occurred, then Fuller would be promoted.[11]

Fuller, in his report to Mouton on November 7th, was high in praise of crewmen aboard his vessel:

> I can not close this report without returning thanks to officers and men. Where all did their duty gallantly, it may seem invidious to mention particular names, yet I must particularly mention the

good conduct of O.S. Burdett, pilot, who for two hours and a half, during the fierce combat on the 3rd instant, maneuvered the boat with the utmost coolness; also the same gallant conduct on the 5th instant. Each of my lieutenants did his duty nobly and ably. Also F.G. Burbank, gunner, and privates F.D. Wilkinson and Henry Dorning deserve particular mention for their gallant conduct. But all did their duty well and are again ready to meet the enemy should they come up and try us again.[12]

Buchanan was resigned to temporarily stopping his attacks at Cornay's bridge until Weitzel's forces of field units could counterattack Rebel sharpshooters that occupied both banks of the bayou. He stated that the *Cotton* was in such a position that she could not escape, and also gave orders to the commanders of his fleet to refrain from shelling as much as possible for the time being as Parrott ammunition was in short supply.[13]

During this period, the *Diana* was very active in making reconnaisances of the adjacent lakes and bayous. One of its services was obtaining timber for Colonel Thomas to repair the bridge at Bayou Boeuf. On the 6th of November, Acting Commander Weeks, while cruising in Grand Lake, heard about some cotton from an "agent, Mr. Todd, who represents himself as a Union man" who suggested that Weeks take the cotton to Brashear City in order "to prevent the Rebels from burning it." Buchanan stated that there were 255 bales which were confiscated and that the owners were Union men who lived in Franklin.[14]

The Todd plantation was located on the bank of American Bayou, across Six Mile Lake, and almost due north of Pattersonville. On another cruise in the lakes, Weeks, accompanied by his captain, George Kendall, stopped at the Todd plantation and confiscated 99 hogsheads of sugar. This was also brought to Brashear City and then shipped to New Orleans. Robert Todd, who was one of the owners of the plantation, was a boyhood friend of Kendall. During a deposition trial following the Civil War it was claimed that Todd was not the owner of the sugar—that it belonged to a William Robertson of New Iberia.[15]

On the 7th of November, Buchanan ordered Acting Master Wiggins of the *Kinsman* to take along the *Seger,* which was captured earlier, and search for two steamers that he had heard were hiding out in one of the bayous that emptied into Grand Lake. After some trouble, Captain Wiggins succeeded in locating the vessels about nine miles up in the narrow Bayou Chevral. He found the steamers grounded and almost useless. One of them, the *Osprey,* had no wheel, and part of her machinery was gone, and the other, the *J.P. Smith,* was rotten.

Wiggins' crew captured a gang on board who were making Bowie knives, molding buckshot and bullets, and also found an order to burn the vessels if they were discovered by the Yankees. Wiggins, however, after consulting with his chief engineer, decided to burn the steamers because the possibility existed that they could be repaired and utilized by the Rebels. The captain of the *Smith,* and a Captain Caldwell along with his group who were stationed there, were taken prisoners and turned over to Colonel McMillan at Brashear City.[16]

On the 9th of November, Weitzel was assigned to a large area which was to be known as the District of LaFourche. This military district included the whole of Louisiana lying west of the Mississippi, except the parishes of Plaquemine and Terrebonne. His headquarters were located at Thibodaux.[17]

The huge salt mine on Petite Anse Island was developed by Judge Daniel Avery to supply the needs of the Confederate States and Army. (Sketch from *Harper's Weekly*)

Chapter 5

THE FATE OF THE COTTON

PETITE ANSE ISLAND (NOW KNOWN AS AVERY
Island) is a small, lofty, and beautiful region that reflects the
handicraft of Mother Nature. This island is located approximately 10 miles southwest of New Iberia, rises about 170 feet
in the midst of a wide sea swamp, and contains an enormous
deposit which was vital to the Confederacy—salt.

Judge Daniel D. Avery, a prominent southerner who was
married to Sarah Marsh, owner of most of the island,
developed the rock salt mine primarily to supply the precious
commodity to the Confederate States and Army. In fact, he
allowed a number of Southern states to establish their own
works on the island, with the mine placed at Taylor's
disposal. The large salt supply enhanced the establishing of a
packing plant at New Iberia to cure beef. Consequently,
large quantities of salt and salt beef were transported by
steamers to Vicksburg, Port Hudson, and other ports east of
the Mississippi.[1]

A Gunboat Named Diana

General Butler, anxious to cut off the flow of these valuable supplies, directed Buchanan to organize a force for the destruction of the Avery salt mine. Around the middle of November, the lieutenant commander ordered the gunboat *Diana*, the gunboat *Grey Cloud* (also known as the *Kinsman*), and the steamer transport *St. Mary's,* which was loaded with McMillan's 21st Indiana Regiment, to proceed via the Gulf of Mexico, Vermilion Bay, then up the crooked Bayou Petite Anse to the island.[2]

The Confederate command received word of the Union movement and immediately dispatched T.A. Faries' Louisiana artillery units to the island with his 3-inch rifles and 12-pound howitzers. After struggling to reach their destination, Second Lieutenant Oscar Gaudet took position on a narrow strip of woods on the sea front of the island with his howitzer section, while First Lieutenant B.F. Winchester stationed his 3-inch rifles on the elevated part of the island.

On Friday the 21st, a small body of Union soldiers began landing in small boats, and, as they approached Gaudet's position, "five spherical case" were fired at the invaders causing them to disperse and retire rapidly towards their boats "dragging with them" a number of their dead and wounded.[3]

On the following day, Winchester's units began returning the fire of the Union gunboats which were visible in the bayou about a mile and a half away. After firing 33 rounds, the battery commander realized that only a few of the shells managed to reach the target area, so he ordered his section to secure a closer position at the bottom of the hill—an effective move which caused the invaders to eventually leave and head out towards the Gulf of Mexico.[4]

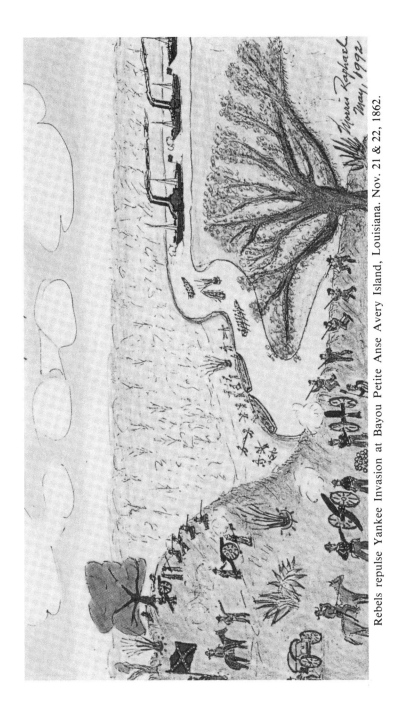

Rebels repulse Yankee Invasion at Bayou Petite Anse Avery Island, Louisiana. Nov. 21 & 22, 1862.

Navigating in shallow Bayou Petite Anse was a chancy operation for the Union fleet. The large vessels made their approach towards the island with little difficulty since they had the benefit of a stiff south wind, but, while withdrawing, the wind shifted to the north causing a low tide and the Union fleet was grounded and stranded in the bay area for a period of 15 to 20 days. They were able to gain flotation only after dumping overboard such supplies as coal, cannon balls, Parrott shells, grape shells, grape shot, and cannisters.[5]

General Butler was ridiculed in a letter written by a New Orleanian which was published in the Cincinnati *Commercial* stating that the salt mine affair was a "hairbrained invasion." Even Colonel McMillan commented in a report to the general that it was impossible to destroy the mine since it was solid rock salt and not brine which had been used in the evaporating process.[6]

On the 8th of November, 1862, General Nathaniel Banks was officially assigned by the President of the United States to the command of all forces of the Department of the Gulf, including Texas, thereby replacing Butler. This department was designated on January 5th as the Nineteenth Army Corps by the Union War Office. Banks had faced Taylor earlier in the Shenandoah Valley campaign where the Yankee brigade was outnumbered and plastered by the Confederate forces under General Thomas "Stonewall" Jackson. But now Banks found himself in a different and rather comfortable position—he would be superior to Taylor in manpower, armament, and gunboats.[7]

Banks encountered delays and did not actually take over his new command until December 17. He left New York with 20,000 men and found 10,000 more in New Orleans including

Union General Nathaniel Banks (Library of Congress)

Union General Cuvier Grover (*Harper's Pictorial History*)

8 batteries of artillery. This was regarded as a pretty strong force, considering that the Confederates were scattered in small units throughout the state of Louisiana. It was evident that Banks had his sights set on the acquisition of the Red River Valley which included the Atchafalaya Basin.[8]

But a few days after his arrival in New Orleans, Banks struck out in a different direction. He ordered an invasion and attempt to occupy Galveston, Texas. Weitzel became quite upset about decisions the Gulf Department command was making which he claimed affected his plans and his four gunboat strength in the Teche offense. He pointed out that one of the gunboats, the *Estrella,* was ordered to Galveston and that Buchanan's flagship, the *Calhoun,* would soon be compelled to go to New Orleans for repairs, and that there were other changes. Admiral Farragut, however, after receiving Weitzel's communication, pled ignorance of the importance of the *Estrella* in the Berwick Bay area and claimed that Buchanan had replied that he could spare the gunboat.[9]

Banks' move to Galveston proved disastrous. On New Year's Day the Union flotilla of two troop-laden transports and six gunboats were bested by Major General John B. Magruder's meager land forces along with two armed steamers which were protected by cotton bales. The Federals lost two gunboats and several hundred men in the encounter. Although the remainder of the vessels had raised white flags to negotiate a truce, the Union navy claimed that firing continued on the banks where a Union garrison was posted. The firing was regarded as a violation of the truce and so the Federal fleet put out to sea making it as best they could back to New Orleans.[10]

While the Texas invasion was in process, General Taylor took advantage of the precious time by training soldiers and strengthening his fortifications. He located a spot in the Atchafalaya Basin which he thought he could develop into a strategic military post. It was a mound called "Butte-á-la-Rose," on the west bank of the Atchafalaya River about 12 miles from St. Martinville. In this area the basin branches funnel into a main channel which passes along side of the mound which is high enough to be protected from flood waters. Taylor had two 24-pounders erected there and called the place Fort Burton.

After the *Diana* returned from the unsuccessful Avery salt mine mission, Buchanan ordered the vessel to resume its reconnaissances in the Atchafalaya Basin. He received information that there were steamers transporting sugar from Lake Fausse Point through Chicot Pass and then on to Vicksburg. Buchanan assigned Acting Master Goodwin to capture the steamboats, and added, as a consort to the *Diana,* a small launch which his naval units had captured earlier. The launch carried a 12-pound howitzer and a small crew of 10 men from the *Calhoun.*[11]

The two vessels navigated to the vicinity of Butte-á-la-Rose where Negroes were interrogated and much information received about the steamboat activity. Assistant Engineer Baird, who was aboard the *Diana,* gave the following report concerning the capture of Rebel steamers:

> The current was swift, the *Southern Merchant* came swiftly down, and as soon as she got fairly round the point, we ran alongside. Everyone jumped on board save one keeper in each boat.

Francis (Henry B. Francis, a master's mate) went to the wheel, armed. I went to the engine, put my hand on the throttle, and said, "Jerry Griffin, I'll take charge for the present," for I had learned his name from the contraband. Jerry said he was glad to see me, called me "old fellow," knew my face well, but could not remember my name. I did not return on board the *Diana,* but Jerry and I stood watch and watch until we reached Berwick Bay on the 10th of December. On the way down the Atchafalaya, and before we reached Grand Lake, we caught the *Naniope.*

The *Merchant* had on board 56 hogsheads of sugar, 4 of molasses, and a few bales of cotton. She had about a dozen shotguns, of which I selected one. The *Naniope* was nearly as heavily laden. Captain Sanders commanded the *Merchant.* He was a Maine Yankee by birth, and by no means a reb; was not yet a pronounced Union man. Captain Deceur (sic) commanded the *Naniope.*[12]

Although Weitzel claimed undisputed possession of the entire country between Boutte Station and Brashear City, he was concerned about the *Cotton* and "the deadly skill with which her guns had been served." He heard rumors that the Rebel gunboat had increased its armament in both caliber and number, and consequently posed a threat upon his forces at Berwick Bay. This worried the Union general to the point where he decided to strike the first blow and do so as quickly as possible.[13]

He concentrated all his troops for the expedition which consisted of the 21st Indiana, 6th Michigan, 8th Vermont, 12th Connecticut, 75th New York, 160th New York, 23rd Connecticut, four pieces of Battery A of the 1st Artillery, two pieces of the 4th Massachusetts Battery, 5th Artillery, 1st Maine Battery, 6th Massachusetts Battery, Company B of the Louisiana Cavalry, and Company B of the 8th New Hampshire.

By utilizing gunboats, Weitzel began transferring his troops across Berwick Bay at 3 a.m. January 13th, 1863. The artillery, cavalry, and infantry then proceeded towards Pattersonville where they disembarked and formed in line of battle. Under the protection of Buchanan's fleet of the *Diana, Estrella, Kinsman,* and *Clifton,* Weitzel moved his brigade to Lynch's Point which is located at the junction of the Teche and the Atchafalaya.[14]

On the following day, all units struck out with the firm intention of eliminating their nemesis, the *Cotton,* which was spotted above the obstructions with its bow and guns faced downstream and ready for battle. The Union plan of attack was for the fleet to proceed up the bayou blasting away while the infantry was deployed on both banks to combat the Rebel pickets and, at the same time, protect its gunboats.[15]

The *Diana,* which had transferred some of the troops upstream, was ordered to cross the 8th Vermont Regiment to the northern bank of the bayou and, if possible, to pass through the obstructions at Cornay's bridge. The Teche is a crooked stream and in this particular section it flows in a rather eastwardly direction.[16]

The gunboats were so large that they had to proceed single file with the *Kinsman* leading, the *Estrella* next, the

Calhoun, and then the *Diana.* A hot exchange began at around 9 a.m. with the *Kinsman* and *Estrella* engaging the *Cotton.* The Union artillery joined in.

Rebel First Lt. B.F. Winchester, who was in command of Faries Battery, arrived just in time to protect the *Cotton* whose gunners were being swept away from their posts by Yankee gunfire. He deployed three sections of artillery. In his left section were two 12-pounder bronze field howitzers. In the center were two 6-pounder bronze smoothbore guns which were transferred to the north bank to assist Colonel Leopold Armant who was in command of the Eighteenth Regiment of the Louisiana Volunteers, and in Winchester's right were two 3-inch Parrott rifles. On the north bank, near the obstructions, were numerous rifle pits occupied by the Rebel infantry and as soon as the *Kinsman* neared the obstructions, it received heavy shelling from the *Cotton* and the riflemen.[17]

Though Captain Wiggins of the *Kinsman* returned fire, Rebel sharpshooters caused his men to lie flat on the deck. His executive officer was wounded by a minie ball and his vessel was struck five times from the *Cotton's* shelling. As he maneuvered his gunboat to get out of range of the rifle pits, a torpedo exploded under his stern, leaving him helpless and vulnerable to shellfire from all directions. He finally managed to retire out of action and, as he navigated downstream, he was followed by the *Estrella.*

Buchanan, evidentally angered by the *Estrella's* withdrawal, advanced the *Calhoun* hastily to the front position, where he exposed himself carelessly and was killed by a shot from the rifle pits. Suddenly there was chaos. The commander of the *Diana* delivered the startling message that

Buchanan was killed, the *Calhoun* was aground, and if the rifle pits were not cleared out in five minutes, the vessel would be lost.

The Union land forces then stepped up their attacks with the 8th Vermont clearing out the rifle pits on the north bank, the 75th New York clearing the south bank, aided by other infantry regiments, cavalry and artillery. They blasted away at Rebel sharpshooters and the *Cotton.*[18]

Acting Third Assistant Engineer Baird of the *Calhoun* made these interesting observations in his diary:

> I was then standing beside Buchanan on the upper deck in front of the pilot house—the *Estrella* was an iron vessel with sides heavy enough to stop a musket ball, and at least conceal her men. It was the intention of Buchanan, as he said to me, to force the obstructions and follow up the steamer *Cotton,* so he ordered Captain A.P. Cooke (Lt. Cmdr. aboard the *Estrella*) to go ahead up to the obstructions and Cooke replied, "The rifle pits line the shore," but made no move. The *Estrella* was then drifting down. Buchanan then said, "Then move out of the way and I will go."
>
> The *Calhoun's* forward and after decks were flush, no bulwarks except right on the bow at the anchors; her guns were necessarily exposed. Mars (the engineer) was working the engine wheel slow, under one bell; the helm was a little a-port. Buchanan held the spyglass to his eye, looked at the obstructions, repeated what he saw, and told me to verify, which I did. So well do I remember

the wreck of the bridge, the little steamboat, the
flatboat load of bricks, the big logs that looked
like oak, etc.

Directly, the reports of rifles from the pits,
probably 150 feet away, rang out. Buchanan ex-
claimed, "Oh, God!" The glass went over his
shoulder. I suppose in his effort to raise his hands
to his head he had thrown it. He fell like an ox,
and as he fell, I saw a blood spot the size of a half
dollar in front of his right ear and from it, the
blood began to flow. . . . They had wounded the
handsome Foster, Lewis, Perkins, Adams,
Williams, Riley, and May. A spent ball hit my
leg.[19]

The bloody battle raged and casualties mounted on both
sides as the day wore on. The Confederates were startled to
learn that three enemy regiments were advancing in such a
manner that their extreme left threatened to flank the *Cotton.* Upon receiving this report, the *Cotton's* springs were
cut and the order given for the vessel to withdraw upstream
in line with its land forces.

But the Union's heavy gunfire "volley after volley" upon
the *Cotton* proved disastrous in lives and destruction. Naval
Lieutenant Henry Stevens of the *Cotton,* who was heralded
as "fighting like a hero, brave as a lion, and immovable as
the very statue of silence," was killed. And almost
simultaneously, the brave Captain Fuller, who blasted away
at four powerful gunboats, was shot in both arms. A Texas
newspaper account stated that Fuller with "the purple tide of
life gushing from his wounds, stood like granite at his post,

The courageous Captain Fuller of the gunboat *Cotton,* though wounded in both arms, managed to work the wheel with his feet as he backed out of action. (The author adapted his sketch from an original illustration by Kate Ferry)

nor left it until his boat was moored inline" with his troops. Despite his courageous resistance, the gunboat was shot up and there were many casualties. The wounded Fuller then worked the wheel with his feet as he backed the vessel out of action.

Other Rebels killed were Corporal V. Gautreau; Privates J.A. Chestnut, O.A. Fleurat, and J.B. Melancon. Among the wounded were Lt. E. Montague, Sergeants F. De la Rue, J. Gautreau, and D. Como; Privates J.C. Bishop, R.J. Hawkins, F. Devillier, and J.A. Hickman. Colonel J.A. McWaters of the 2nd Louisiana Cavalry was also killed and there were other casualties.[20]

Fuller was removed to the steamer *Gossamer* and transported to Franklin where he was treated for his wounds. Lt. E.T. King assumed command of the *Cotton.* Here again bravery was exhibited as King moved towards the scene of action where the gunboat received another bombardment. Late in the day, the vessel withdrew upstream about two miles to Bisland where it docked for the night. General Mouton, concerned that the obstructions at Cornay's bridge were being cleared, needed more time to complete his fortifications at Bisland. He ordered King to take the *Cotton* back down the bayou and to sink and burn her in such a way that it would be a major obstruction for the Union fleet. But Lt. King, who had sentimental feelings for the vessel, remonstrated against doing this on the grounds that he had risked his life to save the boat and that it was vitally needed in the Teche campaign. However, he reluctantly followed the General's orders.

King had the guns, ammunition, and everything of value removed from the boat and took one pilot, watchman, mate, one soldier, and began what he described as "the funeral trip down the bayou." He then ran the vessel's bow ashore within 150 yards of his enemy's camp, positioned her squarely across the bayou, and had holes cut in the bottom. After the 250 foot vessel sank sufficiently, it was set afire and it "burned like a flash." The small crew made its escape in a skiff and returned safely to Fort Bisland. [21]

This all happened around five o'clock on the morning of January 15. According to a Union report, one of their sentinels came galloping along the forces shouting that a fire-raft was coming down the bayou. They were aroused from their sleep and soon found out that the *Cotton* was on fire. It was stated that "she made a magnificent flame with ever and anon the shells upon her bursting." [22]

The proud General Weitzel was quick to report to Banks that "the Confederate States Gunboat *Cotton* is one of the things that were." He mentioned that his losses were four killed, 14 wounded, and that 50 prisoners were taken. In a directive to his adjutant general, Col. Richard Irwin, Weitzel stated that since the object of his expedition had been accomplished, he ordered his forces and gunboats to return to Brashear City while he retired to his headquarters at Camp Stevens near Thibodaux. [23]

While the Yankees were marching back through East St. Mary Parish, an exciting incident occurred. Elated with victory, the soldiers became undisciplined, fell out of column, and began foraging. Some entered a plantation and began shooting and chasing chickens and turkeys. Lt. Col. O.W. Lull, who was the Union provost marshal, had the mauraders driven back to the road, except for a "long-legged Indiana boy" who disregarded the loud command of the colonel, and continued to chase and beat a huge turkey. The incensed mistress of the place came out with a buggy whip and waded into the culprit. The colonel raised his revolver and sent a bullet through the soldier's regulation hat and said, "Stand still, my man, I'll shoot lower next time." The forager abandoned his booty, fled through a fence, and disappeared in one of the columns.

The southern matron was profuse in her thanks to the colonel, and, as a token of her gratitude, begged him to accept the turkey, which was almost dead. Col. Lull was delighted to receive the gift, which he transferred to the orderly's saddle-bow and the column marched on to its destination. (In 1975, the author received a delightful letter from 92-year-old John Parkerson who told the same story, and that the mistress who waded into the Yankee was his great-grandmother.)[24]

The guns, which the Rebels removed from the *Cotton,* were mounted on wheels and were converted to a siege battery. This consisted of two 25 and one 32 smoothbore, old style cannons, and one 30-pound rifle Parrott gun. The unit, which was placed under the command of Lt. King, was utilized in future engagements. At first, it was called Fuller's Bull Battery because it was so heavy and bulky that it took oxen to pull the guns. Later, the unit became a part of King's artillery.

In the meantime, Captain Fuller recuperated, and through the aid and cooperation of Governor Moore, he was given command of two fine steamboats, the *Mary T* and *Grand Duke.* He moved the vessels to Washington, Louisiana, where he had them converted into cotton-clad gunboats.[25]

A southern matron lashes out at a Yankee who tries to steal one of her turkeys. The Union provost marshal came to the lady's rescue. (sketch by the author)

Chapter 6

CAPTURE OF THE DIANA

IN EARLY FEBRUARY, GENERAL BANKS BEGAN TO
place more emphasis on his Bayou Country campaign. In his
communiqués to Major General Halleck, he indicated that
his chief plan was a movement "by the Bayou Plaquemine
and the Red River and the Mississippi." He wanted the Rebel
fortification of Butte-á-la-Rose, which is located at the junction of the Atchafalaya River and Cow Bayou, to be reduced
by the forces of Brigadier General William H. Emory. Banks
pointed out that if this offensive proved successful it would
"enable us to cut off supplies by the Red River, and to com-
municate with the forces below Vicksburg."[1]

He mentioned that Butte-á-la-Rose was the terminus of a
road from St. Martinville, and, since Weitzel was moving on
the Bayou Teche to intercept the Rebel forces at Franklin,
the possibility existed that Emory and Weitzel could join
forces via the St. Martinville road, and perhaps move upon
New Iberia for the purpose of destroying the saltworks in
that vicinity.[2]

Banks recognized that water transportation was essential in the expeditions and, as a consequence, the gunboat *Diana* was ordered to resume its reconnaissances. On one such trip, the command of the *Diana* reported that all routes from Indian Village (present day Charenton) to Lake Chicot were blocked by drift for a distance of five miles and that Grand River was choked. Since this route of attack proved impractical, Banks urged the operations proceed by way of Berwick Bay to Grand Lake. This was in fact a plan suggested by Weitzel in the first place. Weitzel, who was conducting a comprehensive study in preparation for an invasion, had the *Diana* and *Kinsman* make reconnaissances together and report on conditions along the south shoreline of the lake for landing of troops.[3]

He learned that a vessel drawing six feet could get no closer than three miles from shore, while a gunboat, like the *Kinsman* which drew four feet of water, could get within a mile. But, by the use of flatboats, his forces could maneuver within 100 to 200 yards from the shoreline. Since the lake had a hard bottom, he saw no problem for the troops to wade ashore along with transfer of military equipment.[4]

The crew aboard the *Diana* captured one of Fuller's Negroes who stated that there were three guns at Butte-à-la-Rose manned by members of the *Cotton's* crew, and supported by four or five companies of infantry. It was also learned from Lt. Commander A.P. Cooke of the *Kinsman* that all points along the lake shore were strongly picketed, and at Indian Bend, he noted three 24-pounders in position.[5]

From time to time, the Federal command received reports from contrabands, Yankee sympathizers, and deserters, regarding Rebel activities. Although much of the

Federal gunboats maneuver in the vicinity of the Brashear City docks. The vessel in the center is believed to be the *Diana*. (*Frank Leslie's Illustrated Newspaper*)

information was speculation and exaggeration, there was some that was accurate and informative.

An interesting story is told about a Spanish music man who resided in St. Mary Parish and became a spy for the Union army. Benito Monfort arrived from Cadiz, Spain, in 1859, lived in New Orleans for about six months and moved to Attakapas where he taught music.[6]

Because of an upcoming Louisiana militia law which required residents to enlist for a year, he was determined to make his escape. But, before he did this, he dined with Brigadier General H.H. Sibley who had reported to Taylor for assignment in the Teche campaign. Sibley was an alcoholic, and Monfort drained him of pertinent information regarding troop activities, munitions, armed locations, and gunboats.[7]

In late February, when Monfort made it to the Union lines, he was examined by Brigadier General James Bowen, who was Provost Marshal General in New Orleans. The Spaniard mentioned among other things that he saw two new batteries at New Iberia which had just arrived from Alexandria, and that there were six brass pieces in each battery. He reported the Rebel regiments in St. Mary Parish, excluding the two new batteries, numbered around 3,000 men. The gunboat *Hart,* which was being beefed up in New Iberia, was spotted and her machinery was protected by railroad iron. He mentioned the country as being destitute of provisions and believed troops there would starve within three months time. Monfort also submitted his sketch showing the locations where the troops were stationed. Weitzel and Bowen believed Monfort's statements to be true. The Spaniard had lived at Indian Bend (Irish Bend) for two years and, under

After Federal forces confiscated cotton, sugar, and other items, they were shipped by rail from Brashear City to New Orleans. (*Harper's Weekly*, 1863.)

the prevailing circumstances, his intention was to make his exit to Havana.[8]

Companies from various Union regiments oftentimes accompanied the gunboats on their missions. On February 23, Company B of the 114th New York Volunteers was on board the *Kinsman* for a night picket up Grand Lake when suddenly the vessel struck a snag and began to leak. Lt. J.C. Oltman, assistant U.S. Coast surveyor, stated that a log or snag struck the steamer on her starboard side, forward of the wheelhouse, with the wheel striking very hard against the log. The vessel began to take on water and the the crew engaged in a bucket brigade. But, as the water level in the hold began to rise, Captain Wiggins turned the boat around and started back to his dock at Brashear City. Under the greatest possible pressure of steam, he tried desperately to reach the flats below the Brashear City wharves, and ran the steamer ashore until her bow grounded in three feet of water.

Probing with a 15-foot pole, they found no bottom at the stern. The captain ordered a line brought out from the boat's starboard quarter "to haul her broadside to the bank." But before this could be accomplished, the *Kinsman* filled and slid backward from the bank. It sunk in about 18 fathoms of water at twenty-five minutes past midnight, February 24. Although the *Estrella, Diana,* and *Calhoun* were called in to assist, they were unable to save the vessel, but more importantly they succeeded in rescuing the soldiers and nearly all of the crew. However, five of "the brave" crew members drowned.[9]

Earlier, General E. Kirby Smith had been assigned to command the Confederates' Southwestern Army which included the Trans-Mississippi Department. His responsibility included the state of Louisiana, west of the Mississippi River. Smith was a West Point graduate and a hero in the Mexican War. Later he served in the Indian campaigns on the Texas frontier and, during the War between the States, he had displayed great ability at Manassas and in the Kentucky campaign. He assumed control of the Trans-Mississippi on March 7th and established headquarters at Alexandria, Louisiana.[10]

In late February, Emory's command returned to Carrollton (near New Orleans) to await whatever transportation was necessary in order to carry out the movement west of Berwick Bay. In the meantime, Weitzel continued his reconnaissances of the lakes, bays, rivers, and bayous.[11]

On March 27, 1863, the gunboat *Diana* embarked on a mission which was not altogether considered official business. The stout little steamer, armed with two 32-pound broadside guns, a Parrott and Dalgren brass-pieces, steamed up the Atchafalaya towing two capacious barges. One of the crewmen carried a document which was purported to be a bill of sale for a large amount of sugar which was to be acquired from the "Widow Cochrane."[12]

The *Diana* docked near the widow's sugarhouse which was located below Pattersonville, and the crewmen began rolling hogsheads of sugar aboard one of the barges. Madame Cochrane, after examining the bill-of-sale, cried out that the document was a fraud. Meanwhile, Captain Thomas Peterson of the *Diana* began to suspect that there was Confederate plotting involved in this sugar speculation as the Rebels and the captain's pickets began skirmishing on the Cochrane grounds.

Captain Peterson feared an attack. Although 20 hogsheads of sugar had already been loaded, he ordered that the sugar be returned to the widow. Immediately thereafter, all hands were piped aboard and the *Diana* steamed towards Brashear City, just in time, avoiding a well-planned ambush.[13]

The following day, Weitzel ordered the *Diana* to make a run of the Grand Lake area. The vessel was to plunge down the Atchafalaya to the mouth of the Teche and return by the same route. A detachment of 29 men from Company A, 12th Connecticut Infantry, and 40 men from Company F of the 160th New York accompanied the steamer on the detail.[14]

The Federal command was worried about a strong concentration of enemy troops in the lake area as there were rumors that 300 Rebel infantrymen and two field pieces were stationed on a small island in the vicinity. Weitzel sent his aide-de-camp, Lieutenant Pickering Dodge Allen, to gather whatever information he could from the Negroes along the way. But one main reason that Weitzel sent Lieutenant Allen on the cruise was to make sure that Captain Peterson did not deviate from the general plan. Weitzel's opinion of Peterson was that the captain was inclined to be rash and needed some assistance in judgment.[15]

The bill-of-sale episode was said to be a fraud set up by "Rebel spies who lurked within the Union lines" trying to lure Yankee vessels into a trap. Although the *Diana* succeeded in getting away safely on its first visit, the Rebels eagerly waited and hoped for its return. They laid in wait along the Atchafalaya in the vicinity of Pattersonville hidden in different sectors. These troops included Colonel Henry Gray with several hundred infantrymen of the 28th Louisiana,

Waller's Texas Cavalrymen (who were remounted after their earlier swamp disaster) under command of H.H. Boone, and Lt. Nettles and Captain Joe Sayers with five brass pieces of the Valverde battery.[16]

It may be well to mention here that at Berwick Bay, in the general direction across from Fort Buchanan, there are two routes for vessels to take if they wish to navigate in a westerly direction—the Atchafalaya River, or the Grand Lake route. If a vessel chose the upper route along Grand Lake, it would reach an intersection with the Atchafalaya River about six miles distant. Then, if it plunged down the river past the mouth of the Teche, past Pattersonville, and on eastward, it would wind up back at Berwick Bay. It would have made a complete loop, encompassing a large, swampy, and wooded area, which is actually an island (see map page 61).[17]

As the *Diana* made its run, reconnoitering the lakes, the Rebels watched intently in their hideouts, hoping she would navigate in their direction. They could spot the gunboat far across the island, and watched its movement as it left a tell-tale trail of smoke. But as the day wore on, they were getting impatient, especially since it appeared that the vessel was headed back to Brashear along the lake route.[18]

But someone aboard the *Diana* said, "Supposing we go around by Pattersonville and give the Rebs a shot or two." Another laughingly stated, "And stop at the Widow Cochrane's!" As others joined in, this was all Peterson needed. The gunboat was turned around and headed down the Atchafalaya, past the mouth of the Teche, which was in direct violation of Weitzel's orders. Lt. Allen, trying to discourage the captain, asked what would he do if he were suddenly attacked by a Rebel battery. He replied that he was not afraid of any batteries they had, and that he could blow any of their units to pieces.[19]

About an hour later, as the *Diana* was approaching Pattersonville, Peterson spotted a body of Rebel cavalry and one or two sections of light artillery on shore. Although Lt. Allen advised Peterson to turn back and avoid a conflict, the captain disregarded his protest, and when in range opened fire upon the Rebels with his powerful 30-pound pivot rifled gun, killing and wounding a half-dozen cavalrymen. The Confederates replied with their light batteries in a raking position upon the vessel, accompanied by 300 dismounted Texas riflemen, who "showered their leaden hail" upon the Yankee gunmen who were completely exposed on deck. Since all guns of the *Diana* were located on her bow, the Texas sharpshooters picked off every man who dared to expose himself. A special correspondent of the *Boston Traveller,* who wrote a detailed account of the bloody engagement, stated that "The Rebels imitated the strategy of General Weitzel as he exhibited it in his attack on the Rebel gunboat *Cotton.*"[20]

As the *Diana* retreated slowly down the Atchafalaya, a "fatal bullet completed its errand of death, and Captain Peterson, who was standing in the pilothouse, rushed out and shouted, 'Great God! They have killed me,' falling a lifeless corpse on the deck." Lt. Allen then assumed command of the *Diana* as he slowly retreated down the river towards Berwick Bay. The Rebels, fearing their prize was about to escape, stepped up their firing with good execution of artillery and rifles.[21]

The grape and cannister volleys completely cut away the bulwarks of the *Diana.* One shot penetrated the escape pipe, which enveloped the boat in scalding steam, making it impossible for the crew members to distinguish any object. Because of the dead and dying and the constant firing, Lt. Allen found it impossible to get his sailors to stand by their guns, and the infantry was powerless for fear of exposing themselves to the raking fire. Many sought protection between decks and took shots intermittently.

The officers caught hell! Lt. Dolliver was killed. Lt. Allen was shot along with two infantry lieutenants. Captain Jewett was the next victim. Lt. Hall commanded the vessel until he fell. The dead and dying were strewn across the decks. A plunging shot, which penetrated the double casemating, crashed through the pilothouse, and Enfield bullets perforated the iron sheathing. A fireman had one leg cut smoothly off, a boatswain's mate received a shot which tore the bones of both legs completely out. McNally, one of the engineers, was killed by a fragment which came crashing through the engine-room from a shell that had exploded in the wheelhouse. Scalding steam began to fill the space below where the men were fleeing for shelter.

The bloody battle raged on for nearly three hours. Lt. Harry Weston, last to command the ill-fated vessel, tried desperately to run the gauntlet, as he continued backing his unmanageable vessel slowly downstream in the crooked bayou for a few miles, only to be followed by the Rebs who continued their deadly fire at close quarters. Since the stern was unprotected, the bow was maneuvered to face the gunners as much as possible. The trim *Diana* was said to be unrecognizable at this stage. "The upper works were riddled like a sieve from stem to stern. Every berth was cut in splinters. Chairs, tables, knives and forks, books, broken glass and china, shattered panels, blood-wet beds, and pools of gore—and the dead and wounded—were everywhere."[22]

The exultant Rebels, who were beginning to feel a taste of victory, grew frantic as they yelled and shouted along with the clap of howitzers and the crack of rifles and revolvers.

After tiller ropes and connecting wires were severed by shot, a Mr. Dudley, who was pilot of the gunboat, resorted to what was called the fighting wheel as he tried to back down by the boat's wheels since the rudder was shot away. While he was standing on the ladder, giving instruction to the engineer as to which wheel to use, a solid shot cut the ladder in two and he was knocked overboard.[23]

Since Dudley was a Louisianian, he feared that if the *Diana* were captured, he'd find himself in a very unhealthy situation—he would be hung. As soon as he surfaced, he saw the white flag of surrender on the vessel. Three Negroes jumped overboard and joined Dudley as they swam to safety to an island which was about a mile distant.[24]

At the sight of victory, the Rebels went wild. The lifeboats aboard the *Diana* were riddled with bullet holes, but the Confederate officers managed to make it to the gunboat in sugar coolers. (Sugar coolers were coffinlike boxes used as syrup receptacles on sugar plantations, but were modified in some cases by the Rebels to be used as boats to accommodate one or two persons.)

Acting Captain Weston then surrendered to Major H.H. Boone of Waller's Texas Battalion. It may be well to mention here that this was the same group of Waller's horsemen who were demoralized earlier in the campaign when they were trapped in the St. Charles Parish swamp and forced to leave their horses behind. By this outstanding action of the capture

The Federal gunboat *Diana* is captured.
(From a sketch by Chestee Harrington)

of the *Diana* they had redeemed themselves and were proud of the victory.

One of the Texas rangers who couldn't wait for transportation swam to the *Diana* and let out an Indian war whoop. The Texan grabbed a violin which belonged to Chief Engineer Lieutenant Robert Mars, jumped overboard and swam to the bank, where he mounted a caisson and began playing and dancing to the tune of *Dixie.* Then his comrades, overwhelmed with their accomplishment, paddled out in sugar coolers and swarmed aboard the gunboat to celebrate. Momentarily, a jubilant Colonel Waller arrived on board. Two Confederate gunboats, the *Era No. 2* and the *Hart,* appeared and also joined in the activities.[25]

Around two p.m., on that same afternoon (March 28) while the battle was still raging, Captain M. Jordan, commander of the *Calhoun,* heard the heavy firing in the direction of the Teche, gathered his crew and immediately left the wharf at Brashear City to investigate what the roar was all about.[26]

He proceeded the wrong way. He navigated the Grand Lake route, while the *Diana* was struggling for its existence in the Atchafalaya River, just a few miles west of Berwick Bay. The crew aboard the *Calhoun* became utterly frustrated as the vessel ran hard aground at the intersection of Bayou Sorrell. It was hung-up on sunken logs and their efforts to loosen the vessel by backward and forward movements went to no avail.[27]

The crew then ran out hawsers and kedge anchors astern, trying to heave the gunboat into deeper water, but this was also an unsuccessful attempt. The gig, in charge of R.C. Bostwick, was ordered to Brashear City for assistance. At around 7:15 p.m., the four men who had escaped the *Diana,* came on board and told them the sad story of the capture of the vessel.

This depressing news "shook-up" the *Calhoun's* command, for it not only faltered in taking the wrong route, but was now, itself, vulnerable as easy prey to the victory-motivated Rebels. Captain Jordan, in a frantic effort, decided to lighten the ship by throwing overboard coal, anchors, chain, cable, shot, shell, water, provisions, and other heavy objects. In the meantime, he kept his engine constantly working at the kedge anchor. At about one o'clock the following morning, the crew succeeded in getting the *Calhoun* afloat and with a deep sigh of relief, Jordan returned his vessel safely to Brashear City.[28]

After receiving confirmation of the *Diana's* tragic capture, the commander of the *Calhoun* ordered his boat to be "coaled up" and then headed to Pattersonville under a flag of truce. There they would see about arrangements for the dead and wounded, and, if possible, secure the parole of the prisoners. Although the Rebels stopped the *Calhoun* at the head of Berwick Bay, she was later allowed to proceed to Pattersonville. The *Calhoun* succeeded in its efforts and returned with 99 paroled soldiers and seamen—also the bodies of Captain Peterson and Master Mate Dolliver. But three army officers, three engineer officers, and Captain Henry Watson, Jr. were kept as prisoners. Included in the list of prisoners was Lt. Pickering Allen who had suffered a serious bullet wound in the left side of his body.[29]

According to Weston, there were 33 Union men killed and wounded in the bloody engagement—seven of whom were officers. He listed the Confederate casualties as 40 killed and wounded. A contradiction to this account was noted in Charles Spurlin's book entitled, *West of the Mississippi with Waller's 13th Texas Cavalry Battalion.* He stated that the Confederates lost only one man and his death was accidental, while General Taylor placed enemy loss at 150. Taylor also reported that the gunboat was not seriously damaged and that it could be repaired and placed into service immediately.[30]

At this juncture, the Confederates found themselves blessed with several gunboats. These included the newly acquired *Diana* and *Queen of the West;* the *Era No. 2;* the *Hart;* and the ram *Webb.* The *Queen* and the *Webb* were stationed at Butte-á-la-Rose on the upper Atchafalaya.[31]

Weitzel warned Banks that he needed more light-draft gunboats to maintain his superiority in Berwick Bay. He emphasized that he wanted vessels drawing less than seven feet of water. Losing the *Diana* with her heavy guns and ammunition was a serious blow to the Federal fleet. The wounded Lt. Allen, who was respected and loved by his fellow Yankees, and even liked by his Rebel captors, made his dramatic surrender of the vessel at Franklin when he stepped up to Captain T.A. Nettles of the *Diana* and said, "Take care of her sir, and hoist your flag on her." (Soon after the vessel was captured, Taylor placed Nettles in command.)[32]

Later, a strange thing happened aboard the Rebel steamer *Cornie* which had been temporarily converted into a hospital ship. Loaded with Confederate wounded and some Yankee prisoners while enroute to New Iberia, the captain became panic-stricken and returned his boat to Franklin. Lt. Allen then procured a six-shooter in town, confronted the captain, and demanded the surrender of the boat. This good steamer, with nearly one hundred Rebels, fell into the hands of the Federal forces.[33]

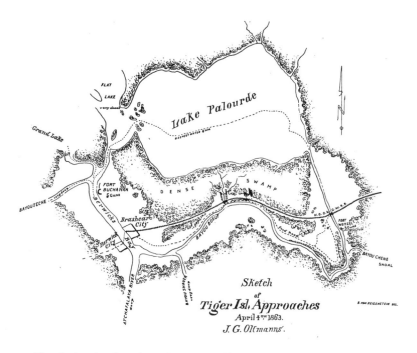

Sketch showing location of Brashear City and Berwick with respect to forts, waterways, swamps, and a railroad line. (National Archives, Washington, D.C.)

Chapter 7

BISLAND

DURING THIS PERIOD, GENERAL WEITZEL
removed his headquarters from the Thibodaux area to
Brashear City, where he was concentrating his command for
the spring offensive. But then, on March 20th, preparations
were made for the "big skedaddle," as his troops called it.
Although there was no specific confrontation, they were
under the impression that they were retreating. First, around
300 sick men from artillery camps and regimental hospitals,
and others unfit for active duty, were loaded aboard a
hospital train at midnight and sent to New Orleans.[1]

Silently, the army wagons began to carry off tents and
baggage. Mules could be seen dragging the heavy cannon
from the fort, and artillery wagons noiselessly trundled over
the soft turf. By daylight, it appeared the whole brigade was
headed by rail in the direction of New Orleans. But it was a
short trip backwards because the troops, after riding eight or
ten miles, surprisingly found themselves encamping upon a
newly ploughed cane field in the vicinity of Bayou Boeuf.[2]

The place, as described by Harris Beecher of the 114th

New York, was "a clearing in the forest, and presented but few attractions. All around the horizon were seen the tall cypress of Louisiana swamps, every branch and limb of which drooped with the weight of a silver gray moss, that hung in heavy festoons to the ground. The only permanent marks of civilization in sight were a few shanties around the railroad station, and a couple of dilapidated sugar mills. The swampy nature of the country, and the severe rains, conspired to make their camp at this place a very disagreeable one."[3]

A correspondent gave this description, "Such mud has existed nowhere else since the ark struck on Ararat. The boys are emphatically stuck in mud on all sides. Mud in their boots, mud in their tents, mud in their water, mud in their food; even the brains of the most astute are decidedly muddled. They eat and drink and sleep in mud, and I believe if they should die in the mud hole, they will become mud-slimy, oozy mud, the favorite resort of cat-fish and alligators. . . . The camp is situated in a cane field, furrowed like corn rows, the stubble from 10 to 12 inches high, the mud ankle deep in all directions, and beautiful little puddles shining on all sides like stars in a chocolate sky. . . .

The rose is red, the grass is green,

But mud like this, I've never seen."[4]

The place took on the name of Camp Mansfield, and a visit from General Banks gave rise to the general impression that active duty was near at hand. Day by day new camps were springing up all over the open fields. "As far as the eye could reach, one could see nothing but white tents and floating flags, and blue forms."

On the wide, open fields, between a levee on the opposite

side of the bayou and a background of trees, stood a large sugar house which was once the depot and storeroom of an extensive plantation. This building, and some adjacent smaller facilities, were selected by the Union command for the troops to store their bulky personal supplies until they returned from their march through the Attakapas country.

Over half a million dollars of valuable items such as trunks, boxes, and desks, which contained money, watches, jewelry, confiscated articles, along with other valuables were deposited. Also, bales of clothing, muskets, and rifles were piled to the ceilings. Enlisted men from several regiments were stationed to guard the buildings. (Ironically and unfortunately for the soldiers, their stockpile was purposely set afire by their own command as the Yankees, in later action, beat a hasty retreat through the area. This was done in order to prevent the Confederates from confiscating the precious items.)[5]

The retreat from Brashear City was said to be a strategic move by the Federal command to throw its enemy off guard, while, at the same time, the big build-up of troops was made without detection. According to Yankee reports, the Confederates were completely deceived, and ceased to work on their fortifications. On April 2nd, the Union army was thrown forward into Brashear City again. At Bayou Ramos, troops left the track and moved on a road that ran along Yellow Bayou. A brigade hospital was established across the Atchafalaya on Cow-pen Island, a mile below Brashear City.[6]

The Confederates under "Dick" Taylor were stationed in the Franklin-Bisland area with an effective force of 4,000 men. The Union plan of attack was to deploy three divisions.

Two of these divisions, under the command of Generals Weitzel and Emory with approximately 10,000 troops, were to attack Taylor's front at Bisland. The other division, under General Grover, numbering around 8,000 men, was to proceed aboard an armed flotilla up the Atchafalaya, and then westerly along Grand Lake to secure a position in the Rebel rear to cut off their retreat and, if possible, capture Taylor's forces.[7]

General Banks and his staff arrived for the impending confrontation, and even planned to be in the front lines where they could work out their strategy first hand. On the morning of April 9, 1863, the Union army, by utilizing its gunboats and transports, began the initial phase of the long awaited invasion, moving troops to the west bank of Berwick Bay. A small party of Rebels who were observing the incursion were driven back, as Weitzel's forces, followed closely by Emory's, landed safely and took a position behind Berwick where they bivouacked for the night. Necessary transportation and supplies were sent over during the night and also throughout the following day.[8]

Grover, who had intended to leave with his flotilla at two a.m. the following morning, was delayed by fog and difficulties in the loading of horses and military equipment. He departed from the Brashear docks at eight a.m. with 8,000 troops jam-packed aboard the gunboats *Clifton, Estrella, Arizona,* and *Calhoun,* and transports *Laurel Hill, Quinnebaug,* and *St. Mary's.* Two small tugs towed rafts and flatboats which were loaded with artillery and munitions.[9]

On April 11th, Weitzel ordered out strong infantry and cavalry forces as pickets with artillery posted in position commanding the roads and woods. The Rebels, who continued to make bold attacks trying to harass the invaders, were met by cavalry companies of Capt. Williamson and Lt. Perkins, as troops skirmished across the countryside.

The order in which the Union forces advanced was as follows: 8th Vermont, Colonel Thomas, extreme right; 114th New York, Colonel E.B. Smith, right center; 160th New York, Lt. Colonel Van Patten, left center; 12th Connecticut, Lt. Colonel Peck, left wing; Williamson's 1st Louisiana Cavalry was in extreme advance, closely followed by skirmishers from the different regiments. Captain Bainbridge's 1st United States Artillery, Company A, and the 6th Massachusetts Battery were accompanied by Captain Carruth. In the meantime, Grover and his flotilla moved up the Atchafalaya into Grand Lake, headed for their planned engagement.[10]

Rebel Colonel Henry Gray of the 28th Louisiana, who was in command at Camp Bisland and also in charge of picket attacks in the Berwick-Patterson area, reported the unfavorable news to Taylor that the Yankees had crossed Berwick Bay and were headed in their direction. Taylor, at this point in time, had his hands full in trying to work out his strategy. He was in the process of expediting his small gunboat fleet at Butte-á-la-Rose to take a defensive position in the vast Grand Lake area. He hurried to Bisland and ordered Colonel Tom Green with his 5th Texas Mounted Volunteers to join Colonel Gray and to skirmish and retard the Union advance.[11]

The slowdown in the construction of Fort Bisland presented a problem. On April 10th, when General Alfred Mouton arrived there, he was distressed to learn that the fortifications were far from being complete. The entrenchments on the west bank were just "thrown up" and the breastworks on the east bank had not even been started. He issued immediate orders for "obtaining hands" and, by the most strenuous efforts, Negroes from the adjacent plantations were collected. Although there were momentary interruptions occasioned by artillery fire from the invaders, the work crew, composed of Mouton's troops and farm hands, worked tirelessly, night and day, to complete the line of fortifications.[12]

On Sunday, April 12th, General Banks and his staff, accompanied by Generals Emory, Andrews, and Weitzel, rode out in front of the troops reconnoitering the country. On one occasion, while Emory was deploying some of his men, Banks rode up and discussed the situation. The two commanders were only three feet apart when suddenly, from the nearby woods, "half dozen muskets were discharged, and the bullets went whistling past and between the generals."[13]

At times, the opposing armies clashed as close as a half mile, until the Union cavalry was hurried forward. In spite of the "volley after volley" firing by the Rebels, the invaders continued their advance utilizing a section of artillery with 20-pound Parrotts.

When General Banks received a report that the *Diana* was spotted, he and his staff rode over to the bank of the Bayou Teche where they saw their "former staunch little gunboat" about a mile away, flying a large Rebel flag. This was Frank Flinn's description of that dramatic moment:

> Everybody wished to take a good look at her, and the consequence was that they remained long enough to hear from her, for a flash, a puff of

smoke, a loud retort, and a whirring, whizzing, whistling noise, the latter becoming each instant more distinct as it approached them, passing over their heads, plunging into the ground beyond with a thud that no doubt sounded musically to every ear, for it was a shell from the thirty-pound Parrott on board the *Diana.* The next instant another gun was fired, this time opposite, from the other side of the Teche. They were the mark that both were firing at, for a shell whistled directly over and lodged in the center of a bank not fifty yards distant, scattering the earth over several soldiers who were resting themselves at the top, and who scampered off in double time.[14]

According to Taylor, the Yankees approached Bisland, or Bethel's Plantation, along the west bank and halted about 1,200 yards from his fortifications, displaying six regiments of infantry in line of battle, three batteries of artillery, and a large body of cavalry. A second line of forces were 600 to 700 yards to the rear. On the east bank, a considerable force of infantry and cavalry, and several pieces of artillery were also in line of battle.[15]

Taylor's forces were positioned in this manner: the 5th Texas Mounted Volunteers under Colonel Green and Colonel Waller's Battalion were both dismounted on the extreme right which rested upon a swamp and commanded the approach by a railroad embankment. The Valverde Battery under Captain Sayers was on the left of Green's command. Col. Gray's 28th Louisiana Regiment occupied the center, along with Cornay's and Semmes' batteries. A 24-pounder

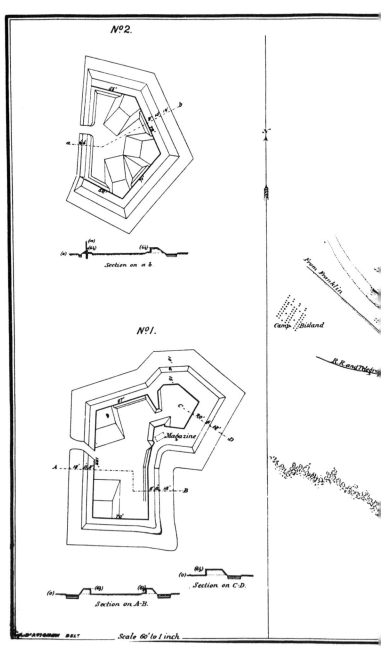

The battlefield of Fort Bisland as it appeared in April of 1863. Redoubts,

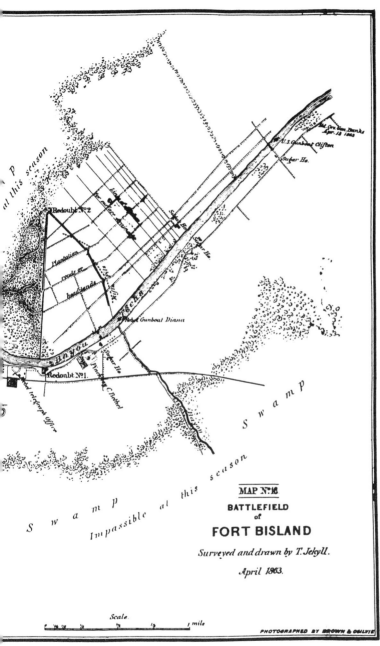

MAP N° 16

BATTLEFIELD
of
FORT BISLAND

Surveyed and drawn by T. Jekyll.

April 1863.

Scale

1 mile

PHOTOGRAPHED BY BROWN & OGILVIE

lines of defense, gunboats, a camp, and other points of interest are
shown. (National Archives, Washington, D.C.)

Union General William Emory. (*Harper's Pictorial History*)

siege gun in position under Lt. Tarleton commanded the road along the west bank of the bayou. The gunboat *Diana,* led by Lt. T.A. Nettles of the Valverde Battery, was active downstream of the line of defenses.[16]

Occupying the east side of the bayou were Lt. Colonel Fournet's Yellow Jacket Battalion, Colonel Bosworth's Crescent Regiment, Colonel Armant's 18th Louisiana Regiment with Faries' Pelican Battery of light artillery, Colonel Bagby's 7th Texas Mounted Volunteers who were dismounted and thrown forward as skirmishers and sharpshooters to the front on the extreme left where the woods terminated in a swamp. Colonel Vincent's 2nd Louisiana Cavalry and Reily's 4th Texas Mounted Volunteers were held back during the morning as reserves.[17]

General Mouton was placed in charge of the troops on the east bank which numbered around 1,500 men, while General Henry Sibley commanded the west side with a force of equal strength. The east line of breastworks was about 900 yards in length. Mouton established a lookout post on top of a parapet in order to observe the movements of the invaders and to be better positioned to command his troops.[18]

When Taylor learned that a Union flotilla had been spotted in Grand Lake moving westwardly, he immediately sent Vincent's regiment along with a section of Cornay's Battery to Verdun's Landing to watch the movement of the vessels and prevent a landing. Verdun's was about four miles northwest of Bisland.

Grover's flotilla continued its movement paralleling the west coastline of the lake. The fleet encountered trouble, however, when the *Arizona,* which was loaded with the 41st Massachusetts Regiment, ran aground at Cypress Pass. The General couldn't wait because he feared it would jeopardize his schedule. He left a few lighters, transferred 400 men onto the *Clifton,* and headed in a northerly direction up Grand Lake. The *Arizona* joined the fleet several hours later.[19]

Taylor, deeply concerned about the fleet movement, again sent Vincent's troops with an additional section of Cornay's Battery to intercept a Union landing which could possibly take place in the Charenton-Hudgin's (sic) Point vicinity. Taylor also ordered Colonel Reily with his Texas cavalry to join Vincent and Cornay as an extra defensive measure.[20]

The Battle of Bisland got off to a rather slow start, but shortly after three p.m. the Rebels opened up with their batteries, with shells exploding in the air, and solid shot ploughing up the earth. General Banks and staff, who had galloped to the front line, appeared calm and cool, as the Rebels' deadly missles filled the air.[21]

Since the *Diana's* gunfire was an effective element in stalling the Union advance, Captain Albert Mack of the 19th New York, with his 20-pound Parrott, was ordered to take a closer position against the gunboat. Although 20 shells were fired at the vessel, striking it several times, she sustained the blows. Furthermore, the gunboat gave a rather deceptive and mysterious performance, as she would appear at intervals, blast away, and immediately disappear. Captain Mack theorized that the vessel was lashed to the side of a dock with a long rope. When the rope was loosened, the boat would maneuver by its steam power to the center of the Teche, fire her guns, and then instantly be drawn back out of sight. The *Diana's* gunners, coupled with the Rebels' rapid firing of heavy field pieces, proved to be an effective factor in holding back the Union advance.[22]

The Yankee front line of attack was under the command of General Halbert Paine and was composed of the 4th Wisconsin, 8th New Hampshire, 133rd New York, 173rd New York, all of which were deployed on the west bank near the bayou. General Weitzel's troops held the extreme left of the west bank's line. The second line was in command of Colonel Ingraham of the 38th Massachusetts. The troops under his command were the 110th and 162nd New York, 4th Massachusetts, and the 16th Vermont. The third brigade was situated on the east bank and under the command of Col. Gooding. His regiments included the 31st Massachusetts and the 175th New York.[23]

According to Pvt. L.B. Bennet of the Wisconsin Regiment, there were three regiments of Indians from Indian ter-

128

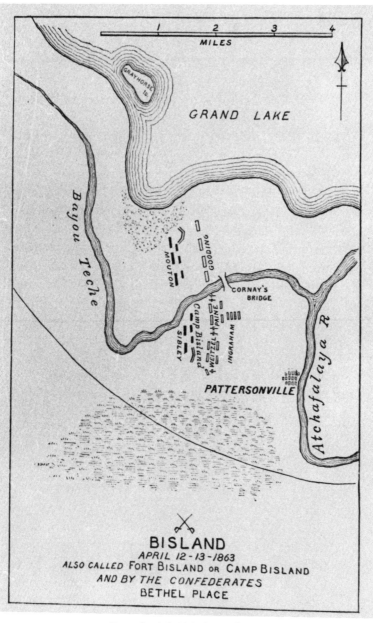

MILES

GRAY HORSE Id.

GRAND LAKE

Bayou Teche

MOUTON

GOODING

CORNAY'S BRIDGE

Camp Bisland

WEITZEL PAINE

SIBLEY

INGRAHAM

Atchafalaya R.

PATTERSONVILLE

BISLAND
APRIL 12-13-1863
ALSO CALLED FORT BISLAND OR CAMP BISLAND
AND BY THE CONFEDERATES
BETHEL PLACE

From Irwin's *19th Army Corps.*

ritory who were fighting on the Rebel side. He remarked that one of the Indians "who appeared to be a chief was the tallest man I ever saw, and I think he must have been eight and a half feet tall."

Some Union troops, which had unconsciously approached too close to their enemy's works and were violently attacked, were ordered to fall back into a deep dry ditch which was parallel to the line. As the day wore on, the battle grew fiercer. The thunder of artillery blended into a continuous deafening roll and as the firing accelerated, it was described as "one of the severest and most remarkable artillery duels of the war. The air was rent with solid shot and grape, while a haze filled the atmosphere from the smoke of discharged guns and bursting shells." A scribe from the 75th New York Volunteers reported that the Rebel fire was "so heavy and well directed as to fill the air with flying iron and mow down the men like grass."[24]

Taylor reported that his enemy made two attempts by charging with its infantry but were repulsed with considerable loss by the forces under Green and Gray. He stated that during these charges the Valverde Battery rendered efficient service. The 28th Regiment Louisiana Volunteers; Col. Gray and Semmes' Battery commanded by Lt. J.T. Barnes; a section of Cornay's Battery under Lt. M.T. Gordy; and Lt. Tarleton's detachment utilizing a 24-pound siege gun, "checked every advance upon the Rebel center and thwarted every attempt to force it." Taylor added that on the extreme right his enemy was not only repulsed but driven back in confusion through the thickets where he sought cover.[25]

Taylor was also proud of the gallant stand made by General Mouton and his forces on the east bank of the bayou. He singled out Col. Bagby's 7th Texas Cavalry, a detachment of the 18th Louisiana Regiment, and Captain Faries' Pelican Battery. He mentioned that Col. Bagby, in spite of a serious wound, remained on the field until his enemy was driven back.

Casualties began to mount on both sides as the battle raged until darkness. During the course of the day's violent activities, it was apparent that the gunboat *Diana* stood out as the Rebels' prime defensive weapon—a fact that the Yankees reluctantly perceived. But time and timing were of the essence. If the Union commanders were to meet their objective in joining forces with Grover and entraping Taylor, it was essential that they destroy the *Diana,* overpower the Bisland fortress, and move on to Franklin. But again, this whole operation depended on Grover's landing and progress at Irish Bend.[26]

Although the heavy firing had ceased at nightfall, the skirmishing continued, and the Union command, taking safety precautions, ordered its front line to retire out of range of the Rebel light artillery. In the meantime, word was received by the Yankee commanders that the Rebels were preparing a warm reception for the bluecoats in the morning.

At daylight, on the foggy morning of Monday, April 13th, General Halbert Paine took the initiative. He very cautiously made a personal reconnaissance close to the Confederate line and learned to his satisfaction that the *Diana* was poised within short range of the Union batteries. He returned with the feeling that his artillery could be positioned in such a way to destroy the Rebels' floating fortress.[27]

But Taylor, who was obsessed with worries, was posed with still another problem. Lt. T.A. Nettles, his brave and

131

capable commander of the *Diana,* became seriously ill. Major Thomas Ochiltree,who was with the Sibley Brigade and on the personal staff of General Taylor, recommended that Captain Oliver J. Semmes and Ed McGowan be assigned to the vessel. Semmes, who was held in high regard by Taylor for his courageous actions, was detached from his battery which was located behind the Bisland earthworks.

According to Ochiltree, McGowan was a rugged and experienced westerner, a former west-coast judge, and one of the organizers of the Arizona Battalion which served the Confederacy. McGowan's outfit consisted of men who had lived on the frontier for years, and to whom six-shooters, Bowie knives and personal encounters were everyday occurrences. Ochiltree, however, made the tough decision naming Semmes over McGowan for the command post of the *Diana.* He felt that since the battery captain was the son of the prominent Admiral Raphael Semmes of the gunboat *Alabama,* he would be well qualified in naval operations. But Ochiltree immediately became concerned when Captain Semmes' first act was to take a piece of chalk and write "starboard" on one side of the deck and "larboard" on the other, so that he would make no mistake in issuing orders.[28]

Taylor had issued stern orders to the officers of the *Diana* to hold its protective position over the fortress until "Hell froze over." Oliver Semmes and his crew fought courageously to hold back the Yankees in what Ochiltree described as one of the bloodiest struggles he had ever witnessed. The valiant team of Semmes and McGowan faced the steady flow of hot shot which poured into the vessel as the firing escalated on that historic morning.[29]

The ditches that drained the sugar cane fields along the

Teche ridge proved to be of vital importance to the Union invaders as the 4th Wisconsin and 8th New Hampshire took positions in close order to the Bisland front. Afterwards, the 133rd New York and 173rd New York were deployed in support of the front line troops. The *Diana* and the Rebels' forces and works were masked by a grove of trees and Negro cabins. But the Union command had the cabins fired so that the smoke would cover and conceal the puffs of the Yankee gunners and impair the accuracy of the Rebel fire.[30]

As soon as the dense morning fog had lifted, General Paine spotted the large Confederate flag and hull of the *Diana* and requested that the heavy guns of the 21st Indiana be sent up to destroy the vessel. Although his request was not immediately granted, Captain Mack approached Paine with two sections of his Black Horse Battery of 20-pound Parrotts. The Rebels continued their brisk fire of shot, shell, grape, and cannister from the light batteries in front and also from the *Diana*. When the vessel changed its position, four companies of the 8th New Hampshire were rapidly deployed along the bayou to fire on her men, and if possible capture the boat.[31]

Captain Mack found the *Diana* to be in easy range of his guns, only 800 yards distant from one side of the bayou, and around 1,500 yards from the opposite bank. Mack's batteries kept up their firing for two hours without cessation—four hundred rounds were fired and two caissons emptied. Just before noon, Colonel McMillan of the 21st Indiana Artillery also found the *Diana* in easy range and fired 20 shots from its 30-pound Parrott siege gun, six of which were said to have struck the vessel with devastating blows. The *Diana's* flag was shot away, and the first shell that struck the vessel

was reported to have passed through her iron plating and
wheelhouse, killing both engineers and three other persons.
Six more of the crew were killed by two other shells, and a
large number were scalded and wounded as one of the shells
passed through a portion of her steam works. The
courageous and battle-worn crew aboard the vessel were
forced to retire upstream to make necessary repairs, while the
fighting at Bisland continued in full fury.[32]

Major Ochiltree, who was dispatched by Taylor to deliver
an important message to Semmes and McGowan, gave this
description of the horror aboard the vessel: "I shall never
forget that sight. Out of the 80 men, 40 lay dead and dying
about the decks. The decks literally ran blood. It was at least
two inches thick all over, and when I came away my boots
were marked with blood as they might have been with mud
after plodding for an hour along a New Jersey road. The
boat was absolutely riddled with shell and shot."

The gist of the message to the commanders of the vessel
was to hold out a while longer and, if they found they could
no longer hold their position, then they were to blow up the
gunboat in midstream so as to obstruct the passage of enemy
vessels.[33]

Later that day Colonel Gooding began concentrating his
3rd Brigade to the extreme right near the woods in an attempt
to outflank the Rebels. Lt. Colonel Sharpe of the 16th New
York succeeded in flanking his enemy but the Confederates
sent forth reinforcements which staved off the attack.
However, Gooding sent more units to reinforce Sharpe, who
made a charge upon a Rebel abatis which was partially hidden in the woods about 200 yards from the earthworks. This
was described as a strong position, as the Rebels had dug a

ditch and felled trees around it. The Confederates, although greatly out-numbered, fought gallantly to hold the fortification, but another strong attack was too much for the meager forces.[34]

Here the Yankees claimed they killed many of the Rebels and captured 86 prisoners including two officers. Although Banks was making gains in his position on the Bisland front, he hesitated to engage in an all-out attack for fear that he would botch up his overall plan. He had not heard from Grover and, as the day wore on, he became worried that the successful venture they had hoped for had miscarried.[35]

But, at around four p.m. a 9-inch shell came hurling through the air from behind the Union lines and burst over Bisland. This was the gunboat *Clifton's* strange way of announcing Grover's successful landing at Indian Bend. The *Clifton,* which had returned to enter the Teche, could not proceed past the obstructions at Cornay's Bridge, but a courier from the gunboat delivered the news Banks was anxious to hear. He was so elated that he had his forces withdraw from the firing line to enjoy a good night's sleep, and cautiously kept a few regiments on duty throughout the night.[36]

Taylor had not heard about the landing to his rear, but the report that the *Diana,* in spite of its shattered condition, would resume its position in the morning was encouraging. But around nine p.m. Taylor received the grim message from Colonel Reily that Grover had landed in the vicinity of Hutchin's (sic) landing at Grand Lake with thousands of troops and artillery units, and had successfully advanced as far as the Teche.[37]

Taylor was shaken by the adverse information. There was

no time for questions. The thought occurred to him that if he had to, he and his small army could cut their way through Grover's division, but he feared losing wagons and supplies. But he had another plan in mind as a last resort. He planned an orderly withdrawal during the night from Bisland. Mouton was ordered to leave the east bank with his artillery and start moving towards Franklin, followed by the infantry with a rear guard made up of Green, his mounted men, and a section of artillery. Semmes was told to speed up repairs on the *Diana* and have the gunboat ready for battle in the morning on the Franklin front.

Taylor lost no time as he dashed off during the night trying desperately to consolidate his forces. He gathered Reily's troops from below the town, and was delighted that Major F.H. Clack's unit, which had been stationed near New Iberia, had arrived in time to support him. These troops were rushed to form a defensive line above Franklin with the artillery paralleling the Teche, and the troops of Reily, Vincent and Clack positioned in a wooded area around a sugar cane field. General Taylor was relieved to learn that Grover had not advanced any further than he had. Otherwise, he would have occupied the field road, including the Yokely bridge, and consequently, Taylor and his forces could have been trapped.[38]

Chapter 8

IRISH BEND

GENERAL RICHARD TAYLOR'S COURAGEOUS
Bayou Country stand was fast coming to a dramatic climax
as he hastened to transfer troops and equipment across St.
Mary Parish. The fact that he was being attacked on two different fronts and outnumbered in manpower about four-
and-a-half to one, apparently didn't deter the gutsy general
as he persisted in making a last ditch effort.[1]

Since the battles of Bisland and Irish Bend were fought
almost simultaneously, the author felt that an account of the
landing of Grover's division above Franklin, and the interesting developments during that particular period would
be beneficial to the reader.

As mentioned earlier, 8,000 troops of Grover's division,
representing three brigades, were jam-packed aboard a
flotilla of vessels which was moving in a westerly direction
along Grand Lake in search of a suitable landing for men and
equipment. The long line of gunboats, transports, tugs, and
flats were under the direction of Lt. Commander A.P.
Cooke, who was assigned to command the naval forces in the
Berwick Bay area.[2]

During the course of the campaign, Grover's troops had become more and more seasoned to the outdoor inconveniences of Louisiana. They had learned, to a certain degree, how to cope with mosquitoes, wood-ticks, cottonmouth moccasins and alligators. Furthermore, they became accustomed to the Bayou Country terrain—the marshy, swampy wetlands, and the network of firm ridges. But, while on sailing expeditions, they were at a loss in distinguishing solid ground from soft, muddy flats.

A first landing was attempted on the afternoon of April 12 at Madame Porter's shell road, but the condition of the road there was found to be muddy and impractical. So they moved on about six miles further to the west in the vicinity of Indian Bend. The name Indian Bend was derived from the tribe of Chitimacha Indians who occupied the area from the lake southward through Charenton, and across Bayou Teche. The Indians here were neutral in their feelings about the war. Although threatened with imprisonment for not joining up with the Rebels, they wanted to be left alone and enjoy the freedom of just going to the lake to fish.[3]

Before daylight, April 13th, General William Dwight, Jr., commanding the First Brigade, sent two of his staff officers, Captain W.J. Denslow and Lt. Oliver Matthews, with a small detachment from the 6th New York Infantry, to examine the Duncan McWilliams plantation road which led from Grand Lake to the Teche. The men found this road to be practicable for all arms.[4]

Vincent's cavalry and Cornay's St. Mary Cannoneers, which were dispatched by Taylor earlier to prevent any landings by their enemy, were having a difficult time trying to keep abreast of the Union fleet. The Rebel units had a long

Landing of Federal Forces at Indian Bend (from *Campfires and Battlefields*)

shoreline to watch and the flotilla moved more rapidly on the lake than the Confederates could by the roads.[5]

Because of the deep draft of the main vessels, the Yankee gunboats and transports were unable to get within 100 yards of the shoreline. But by constructing a bridge of flats, and by the assistance of two very small tow-boats, the invaders began their debarkation at daybreak.

As soon as his leading regiment, the 1st Louisiana (Union), reached shore, Colonel Richard Holcomb threw forward two companies under Lt. Colonel W.O. Fiske as skirmishers, and formed the battalion in line to cover the landing. But, as the troops were crossing a semi-circular shaped clearing, they were met with brisk gunfire from Rebels who were positioned behind a high fence in a nearby strip of woods.[6]

At long last, but a bit late, Vincent's cavalry and the St. Mary Cannoneers had finally caught up with the meandering Union flotilla. The Rebel force was estimated at between 300 to 400 men with a section or two of artillery. But, the Yankee invaders had already gained a foothold and were assisted by the gunboat *Clifton* which raked the shoreline with 9-inch shells.

After Lt. Colonel Fiske was wounded and lost about 15 men, Colonel Holcomb deployed and led five more companies in a rapid attack against the Rebels who realized they were overpowered. They conducted an orderly withdrawal through the wooded area southeastwardly down the McWilliams road. Holcomb closely pursued his enemy until it formed a juncture with its main body of troops which were stationed around a sugarhouse on a large plantation.[7]

Following closely behind Holcomb were Lt. Colonel

Alexander Warner with the 13th Connecticut, Colonel E.L. Molineux with the 159th New York, and Lt. Colonel Michael Cassidy with the 6th New York. Brig. Gen. Dwight of the 1st Brigade was with his force and in full command.

Grover became cautious. He feared exposing his troops prematurely to what could be a superior force. He chose to land all his forces and equipment first, and then attack in an organized manner.[8] He did allow Dwight to proceed with his brigade as far as the Bayou Teche in an effort to prevent the destruction of bridges. But Vincent's forces succeeded, to some extent, in destroying and setting fire to the main crossings which led from McWilliams road into the vicinity of Madame Porter's Plantation. However, after the Union artillery and infantry units gained possession of the junction of the roads and bridges, they prevented further destruction, extinguished the fires, and compelled the Negroes on the plantation to repair the damages.

The Rebels also tried to destroy Bethel's bridge, which was located about 500 yards below Madame Porter's, but were forced to retreat without accomplishing their purpose. However, the Union forces destroyed it later, as a safety measure.[9] Vincent, feeling that he had somehow stalled the Yankee drive, ordered his meager forces to fall back on the road to Franklin where he met Colonel Reily with reinforcements.[10]

Grover became concerned when he learned through his intelligence that Taylor had dispatched a courier to Butte-á-la-Rose ordering the *Queen of the West* and its consorts to move down the lake and attack his forces at Indian Bend. He also learned that besides Vincent and Cornay's troops, another regiment (Clack's) was arriving from New Iberia to the Franklin area to reinforce Taylor.[11]

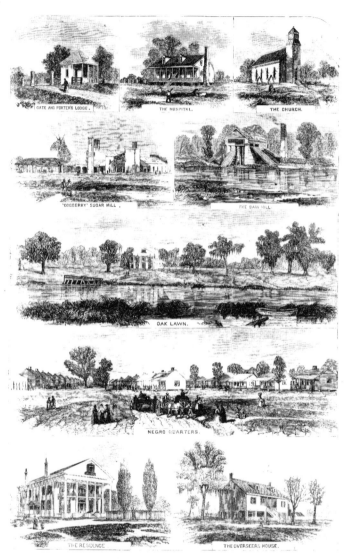

Oaklawn Plantation (*Frank Leslie's Illustrated Newspaper*)

While the Union General was in the throes of unloading military equipment and organizing his attack, he and his troops could hear, at intervals during the day, the thundering gunfire on the far away Bisland front. In late afternoon, Grover led his forces down the rugged field road to the Bayou Teche, crossed over the repaired bridges, marched a short distance past Madame Porter's beautiful mansion (now known as Oaklawn Manor) and planned to bivouac on the nice plantation grounds for the night. The 52nd Massachusetts were deployed as skirmishers, backed up by a section of the 2nd Massachusetts Battery.[12]

The mansion was located about a half-mile north of the main bayou road and faced the Teche. Madame Porter was heralded as the proprietress of one of the richest plantations in the South, owning several square miles of fertile farmlands, a sugar mill, and over 400 slaves. The mansion was placed immediately under the protection of a Yankee unit.

Mrs. Porter, described as a stately, middle-aged lady of fine bearing, bareheaded, jet-black hair, and elegantly attired, appeared to be agitated as she came rushing down the road. She was escorted by a grizzily soldier who carried a musket on his shoulder. She stopped at the stirrup of General Grover who was at the crossroads on horseback, pondering his next move. She had come to intercede with the general on behalf of her son who had just been taken prisoner.

"Please let him go, General," she begged. "The poor boy is quite innocent." She continued, "Please let him go General—he is all I have." She repeated this over and over.

It appeared that the general refused to listen—he never answered a word. The lady's son, a tall, "fierce-looking"

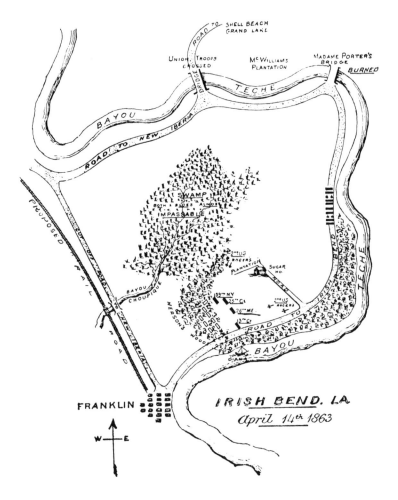

FROM CONFEDERATE SKETCH IN POSSESSION OF COLONEL R. B. IRWIN.

Map of Irish Bend
(from William Tiemann's *The 159th Regiment Infantry*)

young man of about 19 or 20, stood close by under guard. The disappointed Madame Porter was then escorted to her home.[13]

(This interesting section of the country is known as Irish Bend. North of Franklin, the Teche forms a sort of horseshoe with roads on both banks paralleling the bayou. Located at the curved end of the horseshoe is Madame Porter's mansion. The east leg extends in the direction of Franklin, while the other leads to Baldwin. Alexander Porter, who was a U.S. Senator, built the mansion in 1838 and purchased thousands of acres on both sides of the Teche. Porter was an Irishman, as were other prominent settlers in that particular area—hence it became known as Irish Bend.)[14]

As reported earlier, Taylor was in the process of establishing a line of defense around a sugarcane field about a mile-and-a-half above Franklin at the edge of Nerson's Woods. Although his troops, in spite of overwhelming odds, courageously held their enemy at bay on the Bisland front, the Confederate general did not want adverse circumstances to imperil his exodus and vowed, if necessary, to cut his way through Grover's line. Consequently, during the night, he ordered a quiet evacuation of troops and equipment. Wagons, containing quartermaster, medical, and ordnance stores, were started at once on the road to Franklin. Troops consisting of Colonel Green and his regiment as the rear guard, Waller's Battalion, and a rifle section of Semmes' Battery were to begin an orderly withdrawal at daybreak. Colonel Gray with his 28th Louisiana Regiment was dispatched to join with Reily's and Vincent's regiments, Cornay's batteries, and Clack's battalion at Irish Bend. This force was estimated as being around 1,200 men.[15]

Although the crewmen aboard the *Diana* were weary and battered, they labored tirelessly throughout the night, making the necessary repairs in order to navigate upstream and face another battle. The riddled gunboat, whose steam pipes and railroad iron had been pierced by conical shells from Union Parrotts, and splattered with blood and gore from its recent engagements, succeeded in taking its position in time, and in line, with the Rebel forces.[16]

At daybreak, Tuesday, April 14th, the climactic drive got underway as Grover directed his troops down the winding bayou road towards Franklin. Birge's Brigade with Rodgers' Battery led the column, followed by Dwight with Closson's Battery. Barrett and a strong line of skirmishers were out in front. General Grover was aware that about a mile-and-a-half on the Union right was a forest fringed with low cane where Rebels were posted. But, he remarked that he thought there was nothing there but a picket attempting to secure Taylor's line of retreat.

After the head of the column had proceeded a good distance and was about to turn a sharp corner in the road, Birge's skirmishers ran into those of Clack's Battalion—and the battle of Irish Bend began.[17]

A short distance off the road to the Union right was a large sugar-house, McKerall's, which was utilized as a hospital during and after the engagement. In front of the troops was a sizeable open field, with sugar cane about a foot high, and intersected with deep ditches. Rain during the night across the recently plowed field caused the ground to be soft and heavy, making it difficult for the maneuvering of troops and equipment. Further down in their front, skirting Nerson's Woods, was a strong fence, and off to the right was a swampy area which contained Bayou Choupique, or Bayou Yokely, as it is more commonly known.[18]

Birge's 3rd Brigade, consisting of the 13th and 25th Connecticut, 26th Maine, 159th and 91st New York, were all on foot as they exposed themselves across the open field, not knowing that a strong force of Rebels were hidden behind trees, fences and cane breaks. As the 25th Connecticut under Colonel Bissell and the 26th Maine under Colonel Hubbard advanced as skirmishers, they were met with "extraordinary" shelling by the skillful and rapid firing of Rebel artillery. The invaders were further blasted by musketry as Union losses became quite severe.

According to Major Thomas McManus of the 25th Connecticut, the canes of the previous year's crop stood in that particular section where his regiment was deployed, and the Rebels' shots "rattled through the dry stalks, cracking like hail against windows." He implied that his enemy had an immense advantage in position and that "they were armed with smooth bores, every cartridge charged with a bullet and three buckshot, while our regiment was armed with Enfield rifles, and so, the Rebels, man for man, were giving us four shots to our one in return."[19]

The Rebels cheered as a rain of fragments from their shells exploded across the field, and the 25th Connecticut felt trapped as musketry fire grew hotter and hotter. McManus stated that his men were nearing the end of their supply of ammunition, and if the Confederates had charged at that critical time, they could have "annihilated our brigade."[20]

Frank Moore's *Rebellion Record* gave this dramatic account which was published in the *New Orleans Era,* April 29, 1863:

The Battle of Irish Bend (from *Campfires and Battlefields*)

Our loss was quite severe here, being about 70 each in two regiments, the 25th Connecticut and the 26th Maine. But the main body of the brigade was marching up at double-quick, led on by the almost too intrepid Colonel Birge, and soon passed the point where the skirmishers were holding ground against a fire of musketry at not more than 100 yards distance. For some reason, the 91st New York, on arriving at the line of skirmishers, made a halt under cover of a ditch, while the left (13th Connecticut) and center (159th New York) kept marching on toward the enemy. This halting gave the left wing of the enemy a chance to flank the 159th, and he was not slow to take advantage of the mistake. Colonel Molineux (159th New York) now found his regiment in a most precarious position, suffering from an enfilade fire from the enemy's center and advanced left wing. He accordingly gave the order to halt and lie down between sugar cane rows and in ditches, while the firing continued. In this position, he was comparatively safe, and in the meanwhile, the 91st New York, recovering from the error into which it had fallen, and which caused a most serious loss to the 159th, came nobly up to its proper place, and drove the left wing of the enemy from his position.[21]

The 13th Connecticut, which was led by Lt. Col. Alexander Warner and was Birge's own regiment, lost 50 men in the first few minutes of the conflict as it made a daring charge along both sides of the road on the Rebels' right. The Union riflemen had drilled themselves in a unique and effective type of combat, firing three shots per minute while advancing in battle—a tactic which they mastered and found to be advantageous in the LaFourche campaign. This system was likewise used at Irish Bend as the regiment was greeted with rapid fire from the St. Mary Cannoneers, the gunboat *Diana*, and the Crescent City Regiment. The 13th managed to penetrate into a wooded skirt of Nerson's Woods where it succeeded in capturing two caissons, one limber, four artillery horses, swords, muskets, a great quantity of ammunition, 60 prisoners, and a large and elegantly embroidered silk flag bearing the inscription, "The Ladies of Franklin to the St. Mary Cannoneers." The engagement was hotly contested as evidenced by the many dead and wounded who were strewn across the field. Although Cornay and Clack were pressed back, they held their ground and continued to fire away at their adversaries.[22]

When the firing in front of the 159th New York slackened, Col. Molineux gave the order, "Forward, New York!" when suddenly, he was struck in the mouth by a musket ball. The gallant officer fell, and although not seriously wounded, was carried off the field to a nearby farmhouse where he was given medical attention. He wrote a long letter the following day to his sister Anna telling about his lip being sewed up and that he would not be disfigured. He also mentioned that he'd applied for a furlough to return home for 30 days to get a new set of teeth. In that letter, he gave an interesting account of his tragic experience during the day's battle. Here is some of what he wrote:

> I entered yesterday morning a sugar field with

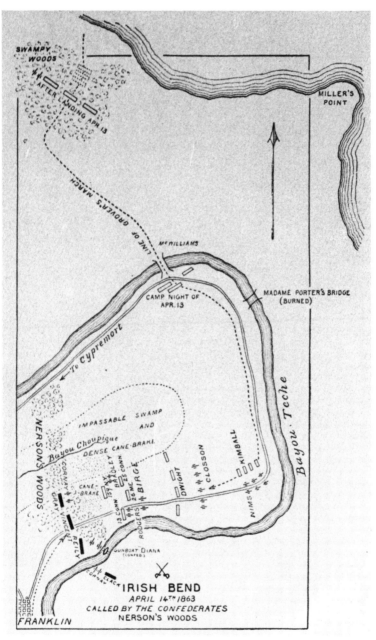

(From Irwin's *19th Army Corps*)

400 men in support of some regiments who were trying to drive the rebels from the woods. I received an order to charge bayonets and drive the rebels out. I obeyed but not being supported properly was outflanked and met with a tremendous crossfire which cut us down in scores. Still the boys followed me but by the time we had reached within fifty feet of the woods, I found in looking back that the line was but a broken mass without unity. I tried to reform them, but it was only murder and then I ordered them to lie down between rows of sugar mounds and fire, this we did for five minutes. It was then I was wounded by a Mississippi rifle ball. I was cheering the boys and was raising on my feet to see how we could best protect ourselves from the rebels who outflanked us. Hardly had I raised on my knees when whack! & I tumbled on my face. The ball entered my mouth tearing away the gums and teeth on the left side, scraped the jaw and out of the cheek....Oh! Annie, my wound is nothing. After I was struck, the rebels on the flank charged upon us as we were lying down. We rose up and resisted them, retreated slowly until the regiment who should have supported our flank long ago came charging down upon them and drove them back. The boys carried me off the field although I told them to leave me, such self-sacrificing fellows I never heard of. About four were struck carrying me off! And among them poor First Lt. William R. J. Plunkett shot through the forehead. Thank God

they think he will live. You must go and give the sad news to his wife. Cheer her up that he will soon be home. In that desperate encounter I lost out of 400 over 100 killed, wounded and missing! The killed and wounded in officers was very heavy. Poor Lt. Gilbert A. Draper shot through the heart. My good adjutant Robert D. Lathrop shot through and through lived but fifteen minutes. Lt. Byron Lockwood shot dead and my brave Lt. John W. Manley, Jr. of Brooklyn the same—wounded.... Harry had his horse shot under him in five places but is well. All died bravely....(from the Molineux papers, Williamsburg, Virginia).

(Molineux resumed command on July 5th. A few days later, he was honored during a ceremony at Algiers, Louisiana, where he presented, among other things, a national flag of silk with heavy gold fringe, bearing the wording, "Irish Bend, La., April 14, 1863." The flag was given to Molineux earlier by the 23rd Regiment National Guard of Brooklyn, New York. The Colonel transferred the Colors to the care and custody of the regiment.)[23]

Presently, Rebel firing escalated to a hot and heavy pitch as the men in gray took advantage of their unique positions. Union forces joined in with shot and shell and, as one of their officers stated, "I never heard such firing. It seemed like a never-ending peal of rolling thunder." But, as the morning sun continued to rise, it became extremely uncomfortable, warmer, and more wearisome for the Yankees. They were not only saddled with heavy rain-soaked packs as they trudged across the muddy field, but found themselves stymied for they were faced with a continuous enfilade of Rebel resistance in nearly every direction.[24]

The *Diana's* effective firing was described by Major McManus:

> Just beyond the woods in the open was the rebel gunboat *Diana*, manned by a crew that had been raised in this neighborhood, who knew every foot of the country, every turn of the bayou, every road, cart path and foot path, every house, barn, negro, mule, and chicken. Emory's force was hastening up from the south, we held both sides of the narrow bayou on the north, and escape for the boat was impossible. The moment the head of our column entered the woods, the solid shot and shell from *Diana's* guns came whistling up the road. We gave them the right of way without waiting for orders; the sidewalk was good enough for us, then. We split into two columns, one on each side of the way, and halted while the general and staff went ahead to reconnoitre. The enemy's gunners began to shell the woods, and such a shelling. We could not return a shot. The *Diana's* guns were far heavier and of longer range than ours, and there we sat and waited while the tempest of solid shot, grape and cannister swept through us and shells exploded over us and spitefully showered their iron fragments on our heads. (From an address by Major Thomas McManus, April 23, 1891).

Pierre Gentieu of Company B, 13th Connecticut made these comments after the war:

The order was given for us to fall back so that the Confederates should advance further in the open field, as we had lines of our troops back of us waiting for the order to charge, and just at that time your gunboat *Diana* began to fire shells over the woods and over their own line toward us. Two of the shells struck in the field on our right, doing no harm, but the third one, by bad luck, struck in our company, passing the back of Robertson, taking his bayonet, haversack and canteen. He was not hurt, but none of the company ever forgot his exclaiming, "Damn, that shell took my four days' ration." The shell kept on, striking the leg off of Krouse on my left, breaking my rifle in my hand, knocking me senseless, and striking Tomlinson on my right in the middle of the body. Killed instantly. If the gunner of the *Diana* is alive yet, he can have the satisfaction that he hit someone that day. (From *St. Mary Franklin Banner Tribune*, April 28, 1959).

The battlefield was littered with dead soldiers and dead horses. Scores of the wounded continuously crawled to the rear where they were carried on stretchers to the make-shift hospital at McKerall's sugar mill. The Union losses of officers and men became so great that it caused disorder and confusion in the ranks. Commands to halt and fall back were heard across the field as regiments withdrew around noon to reinforce and consolidate their forces. This reversal met with resounding cheers and yells from the defenders.[25]

Although Taylor was relieved somewhat that his forces

stood their ground in a show of great defensive action, he was shocked to learn that Colonel Reily was mortally wounded, and was distressed that Colonel Vincent, Adjutant A. J. Prudhomme, Captain R. H. Bradford and Colonel A. P. Bagby were wounded. He stated that all these officers gallantly led their men in battle.[26]

Losses by some Union regiments during the morning engagement were staggering. A Yankee soldier remarked that "the 3rd Brigade seemed to be spent. In that little time, it has lost 320 men out of less than 900 that went in." The 25th Connecticut suffered 95 casualties, which included the deaths of Capt. Samuel Hayden and Lt. Daniel Dewey, as well as the wounding of many other officers. The 159th New York lost 115 men. Lt. Col. Gilbert Draper, Adjutant Robert Latrop, 1st Lt. John Manley, Jr., and 2nd Lt. Byran Lockwood were killed in action. Although Capt. Sprague, Lt. Strickland and Lt. Kinney were wounded, they refused to leave the battlefield. The 26th Maine suffered 68 casualties with Lt. Col. Philo Husey seriously wounded.[27]

Taylor, taking advantage of the lull in the fighting at Irish Bend where he was in command, hastened to the Bisland front, and ordered Mouton to replace him. He then hurried to Franklin where he was to personally direct the wagon trains and troops to move out by a cut-off road, which was apparently unknown to the Union commanders who were rejoicing in the thought that Taylor and company were trapped.[28]

During the night on the Bisland front, the Union pickets reported that sounds were heard indicating some unusual movement behind the Confederate works. Banks gave orders to assault along the whole front as soon as it became light enough to see. That was the morning of April 14th. When the skirmishers moved foward, they found the Rebels had evacuated and, in their haste, left some equipment and stores, which included two disabled pieces of armament—a 24-pounder siege gun and 12-pounder howitzer.[29]

According to Lt. John West, who was in command of the rifle section of the C. S. Light Artillery and attached to Green's rear guard, an orderly withdrawal was conducted. He stated that when his unit reached Centerville, he was ordered to check the Union advance. West masked his pieces while Colonel Green deployed his cavalry, and when the invaders came within close range, they were fired upon, causing the Yankees to retreat through the town behind the cover of their artillery.[30] Action such as this played a great part in retarding the Union advance and allowed the Confederate troops and supplies to funnel their way into Franklin and out on the escape road to Baldwin, Jeanerette, and other points to the northwest.

Taylor, still obsessed with the stark realization that his troops were outpowered and outnumbered, was desperately at work trying to coordinate an orderly retreat from both fronts. After the last Confederate units which were stationed at Bisland had crossed the Bayou Yokely along the Harding Cut-Off Road, General Sibley, who was in command of the brigade, ordered Green to set fire to the bridge. This angered Taylor who claimed that Sibley had not communicated with him and burned the bridge prematurely, thereby jeopardizing the withdrawal of some of the troops at Irish Bend.[31]

Around noon, Mouton received word that Rebel troops from the lower front had retired and that the Union forces from Bisland were approaching Franklin. While Mouton made an exodus with his remaining troops, he was protected

THE WAR IN LOUISIANA—ARRIVAL OF THE STEAMER A. G. BROWN AT TARLETON PLANTATION, BAYOU TECHE, WITH SUPPLIES FOR GEN. WEITZEL.—FROM A SKETCH BY OUR SPECIAL ARTIST, C. E. H. BONWILL.

THE WAR IN LOUISIANA—CENTREVILLE, LA., OCCUPIED BY THE 116TH N. Y., COL. LOVE, SEPT. 28.—FROM A SKETCH BY OUR SPECIAL ARTIST, C. E. H. BONWILL.

Sketches show activities along Bayou Teche. Supplies being loaded on steamer at Tarleton Plantation, and at bottom, Federal troops occupy Centerville. (*Frank Leslie's Illustrated Newspaper*)

by a shield of flying steel from the guns of the *Diana*. When they reached the Yokely Bridge, it was almost consumed by fire, but all the men crossed safely—and in the nick of time.

Grover, in an effort to eliminate the *Diana*, ordered Nims' Battery to be placed in an ideal position to open up on the gunboat, and also deployed two companies of sharpshooters from the 13th Connecticut to pick off the cannoneers. But after Mouton's forces had cleared the Irish Bend area, the brave and heroic Captain Semmes withdrew the *Diana* downstream to the docks at Franklin. There, he set fire to the magazine, swam ashore, and the famous gunboat was "blown to atoms." Unfortunately for Semmes and his crew, they were captured by the cavalry of the 114th New York Volunteers as the Rebels attempted to make their escape across W. P. Allen's field to Bayou Choupique, in the rear of Franklin.[32]

Before Taylor withdrew, he had a number of boats scuttled along the Franklin waterfront. These included three transports, the *Newsboy*, the *Gossamer*, and *Era No. 2*, all of which were used in the transfer of troops and supplies. A large quantity of ammunition and army supplies were also destroyed. Taylor was determined not to leave anything of military value to his enemy.[33]

The Union troops were in high spirits as they pursued the Rebels from both fronts thinking they were on the verge of trapping Taylor and all his men. But they were confused as Yankees ran into Yankees at Franklin and learned, to their frustration, that the Rebel troops and supplies had vanished by the escape route. A note in General Paine's diary indicated that there was such a mixup, a part of Grover's division mistook his unit as the enemy. The Blue Coats became even more frustrated when they found the Yokely Bridge impassable and that Taylor had eluded them completely. Most of the Rebel troops bivouacked for the night in the Jeanerette area about 15 miles above Franklin. Mouton's troops encamped on the grounds of Albania Plantation just below Jeanerette.[34]

About mid-afternoon, Banks, seeing that the bridge could not be repaired before morning, decided to bivouac near Franklin. Grover occupied the Irish Bend battlefield, while Emory held the bayou road between Grover and Banks, and Weitzel the cut-off road.[35]

One of the officers of the 13th Connecticut Volunteers recounted his observations of the dead and wounded on the night of April 14th, following the bloody battle of Irish Bend:

> After my wound had been dressed, I visited the sugar-mill which has been turned into a hospital for both Union and Rebel wounded. Twelve of my company had been hurt—some of them severely, and I wished to find them and supply their wants if possible. The night was very dark and cold. Several hundred lay there. But (only) one or two candles could be obtained, and the surgeons were busy with these. There should have been at least twenty surgeons, but only three or four were present. Some of those worst wounded did not have any attention for several days. Quite a number of dead lay at one door, and a pile of legs, feet, arms, hands, beside the bloody table where the surgeons were still amputating. Nothing was to be heard but

Federal troops enter Franklin.
(From *Frank Leslie's Illustrated Newspaper*)

cries, groans, [and] entreaties. It really seemed as if nobody cared for the sufferers, so few were there to assist them.

Groping a few minutes among the wounded, for the building was pitchy dark, and the ground was covered with victims, I started for a light. It was nearly an hour before I was able to procure the use of one for a few minutes. I soon found my first-sergeant. He had been shot through the neck; yet, as if by a miracle, the wound was not fatal. He was suffering from cold and thirst, and was faint from loss of blood. Throwing my blanket over the poor fellow, I returned to camp and brought him a canteen of hot coffee, and some food for him and my other wounded. Detailing William Patterson, one of our most faithful men, I left, being completely exhausted, sick at heart of war and all its surroundings.[36]

M. C. Rose of Franklin related the story that his grandmother, Mrs. Edmund Rose, whose plantation home was located on the east side of the Teche, had her slaves cross over to the battlefield where they dug a long, deep trench with plows, two furrows wide, where the bodies of dead soldiers were buried. James Hosmer mentioned the burial parties. He wrote that there were "piles of corpses lying by the trenches ready to receive them." He also stated, "Our little battle is known among the men as that of Irish Bend, by others as Indian Ridge. It does not make much of a figure in history. Newspaper reporters were not on hand; but it was sharp, obstinate and bloody."[37]

The ferocity of hand to hand combat was revealed in this

single sentence which was extracted from *Moore's Rebellion Record:* ''The fact that many of our men received bayonet wounds is an evidence of the desperate nature of the contest.''[38]

Chapter 9

THE DEMISE OF THE QUEEN

IN THIS BAYOU COUNTRY CAMPAIGN, APRIL 14TH
proved to be an exhausting day for the Union and Confederate Army and Navy as commanders tried to out-fox
each other, while the men were deployed in heated attacks
and withdrawals. There was another bloody engagement on
that fateful day which played a role in the outcome of the
battle of Irish Bend. As mentioned in the preceding chapter,
Grover learned that a Confederate flotilla, which was stationed at Butte-á-la-Rose, was to move down Grand Lake
and attack his forces. At about 5 a.m., while Grover was
preoccupied with landing his forces at McWilliams' Plantation, Commodore Cooke was alerted that lights were spotted
across the lake and that enemy vessels were headed in their
direction. At daybreak, the Rebel gunboat was recognized as
the ram *Queen of the West*, which was approaching with its
tender the *Nina Simms*. The transports *Grand Duke* and
Mary T, which were loaded with Confederate troops, were
late in getting away and didn't arrive in time. The same
heroic Captain Fuller of gunboat *Cotton* fame was aboard
the *Queen*, and in command of the attack.[1]

A Gunboat Named Diana

(The *Queen of the West* was captured earlier in the campaign by the Confederates at Fort De Russy on Red River. The *Queen* was a freight-boat converted into a ram, and was considered a model of strength and speed. Her hull and machinery were strengthened by timbers and solid wood work, 24 inches thick from stem to stern. The vessel was further protected by two rows of cotton bales, extending entirely around her, including the pilot house, and there was also a layer of cotton upon her deck. The *Queen* was well armed with a bow gun, a 32-pounder rifled Parrott, a 20-pounder

When Fuller's two vessels were spotted at daylight approaching from Chicot Pass, Cooke led his gunboats, the *Estrella*, *Calhoun* and *Arizona* into Grand Lake for a confrontration. (The *Clifton* had been detached earlier to go after the *Diana* in Bayou Teche, but could not proceed to the battle proper because of the obstructions at Cornay's bridge.) As the lake battle began to develop, the *Queen* was out in front with her consort a safe distance behind, while Cooke arranged his boats in a crescent formation, gradually closing in on the *Queen*, and then ordered that firing be commenced at long range.

The *Queen* held her fire until she was about three-quarters of a mile from the Union vessels when she opened up her guns on all three boats. Federal shot and shell were concentrated on the *Queen* from every direction, using a cross-fire pattern of attack. Engineer George Baird, who was aboard the *Calhoun*, claimed that a percussion shell from his vessel struck the roof of the Rebel ram, exploded, cut a steam pipe, and set fire to the cotton which was used for protection around the boilers. Engineers aboard the *Queen* couldn't get

Destruction of the "Queen of the West" by Union Gun-Boats.

Engagement at Butte la Rose.

BANK'S CAMPAIGN IN LOUISIANA.—Sketched by Mr. H. Boese.—[See Page 171.]

The Confederates' *Queen of the West* is destroyed.
Bottom scene depicts a later engagement at Butte-a-la-Rose.

the water pumps started, the boat was ablaze, and 26 of her crew were scalded or burned to death. Baird explained that the *Queen* was armored much like the *Diana* but was different in that the ram was much larger and afforded more room in the casemate for her larger guns.[3]

The following is an account from J. Thomas Sharf's book describing the demise of the *Queen*:

> A cloud of white smoke was seen to rise, as if from the deck of the ram, followed a moment after by a dense, black smoke, and then a sheet of flame. It appears that one of the shells struck and burst in a box of ammunition, instantly setting her upper decks and rigging in a blaze.
>
> As soon as the Federal fleet saw their powerful enemy on fire, her guns silent, and her crew running here and there in wild confusion—some throwing overboard cotton bales with which she was barricaded, while others jumped into the river—all feelings of enmity vanished. Commodore Cooke immediately blew the signal-whistle to cease firing, and assist in rescuing the crew; and as the *Estrella, Calhoun,* and *Arizona* steamed up to the doomed vessel to save and succor those on board of the *Queen of the West*, boats were lowered, drowning men rescued, and all on board the burning ram were transferred to the decks of the gunboats.—95 persons were taken out of the water and from on board the *Queen of the West*; but not withstanding these humane exertions to rescue those on board, it is believed 40 of them were drowned. As soon as

the crew and officers and soldiers were rescued, the ram was abandoned. She drifted about for some time, the flames each moment raging more fiercely until they reached her magazine, when she exploded with a noise which was heard for miles around.

The *Queen's* consorts, seeing the predicament of their flagship, turned around and sped up Chicot Pass and then on to Butte-á-la-Rose.[4]

Following the capture of Fuller and Semmes, they, along with some members of their crews, were taken to New Orleans and delivered to the Provost Marshal at that city. The two captains and 50 other Confederate officers were conveyed to Fortress Monroe. On June 10th, 1863, Captain Semmes, along with McGowan and a large number of other prisoners, while being transferred to Fort Delaware, Delaware, aboard the steamer *Maple Leaf*, suddenly overpowered the guards and made a dramatic escape.

Semmes, Fuller, Captain Eugene Holmes, Jr. of the Crescent Regiment, and Captain J. S. Atkinson of the gunboat *Hart*, which was scuttled a few miles south of New Iberia, planned the seizure of the guard and vessel. They, along with 25 of their fellow prisoners who were from New Orleans, agreed upon a plan that each guard should be surrounded by three men, and, at a given signal which was to be a whistle blast, they would overpower the guard and take away his musket.

After the signal was sounded, a short scuffle took place and the Confederate prisoners took over the vessel. McGowan informed a Lt. Dorsey, who was in command of the guard, of the drastic change of events that had taken

169

place aboard his ship. The Rebels forced a landing along the Virginia coast where 71 of them dashed for freedom and made it safely back to "Dixie." Captain E. W. Fuller, however, was ill and weak, and chose not to escape for fear of slowing down his fellows and jeopardizing their safety. He died while in prison on Johnson Island, July 25, 1863.[5]

Although the Union forces were victorious in nearly all of their engagements in the Teche campaign, it was not as complete as they had hoped. Grover received criticism from some of the Yankee scribes for allowing Taylor to escape, claiming that the Union General had plenty of men, an abundance of artillery, and should have known where every bridge and avenue of escape was located.[6]

There were insinuations that Grover, after landing at Indian Bend, should have directed his troops to Baldwin where he could have "bottled-up" Taylor's forces. It was reported that Madame Porter tried to persuade Grover to take that route, but the General, thinking she was trying to throw him off, took the opposite road towards Franklin instead. Rumors around Franklin that Madame Porter was a Yankee sympathizer were substantiated later during her testimony in the 1872 U.S. Court of Claims for damages and confiscations on her plantation. Her Yankee connections and fraternizations were obvious, considering that her son was immediately set free, her mansion was not burned, and that she went out of her way, far and wide, to wine and dine the officers of many Union regiments during the Bayou Country campaign.[7]

According to this author's knowledge, the losses of the Confederates at Irish Bend and Bisland have never been reported, but are believed to be considerably less than those inflicted upon their enemy. Grover's troops at Irish Bend suffered 353 casualties. These included 6 officers and 43 men killed, 17 officers and 257 men wounded, and 30 men missing. At Bisland, the Union's casualties amounted to 224. These included, 3 officers and 37 men killed, 8 officers and 176 soldiers wounded.[8]

It can be said that "Dick" Taylor was perhaps one of the few generals in history who could boast a victory even though he beat a hasty retreat. He claimed that he never lost "a pot or a pan." As he led his troops in the direction of northwest Louisiana, he scuttled boats, burned bridges, engaged in maurading attacks, and managed to keep out of reach of his adversaries.

On the day following the April 14th battle, the Union troops took off again in hot pursuit of Taylor. But on the next two days march, a Yankee brigadier general described the terrible atrocities committed by soldiers from his brigade. He recounted that the scenes of disorder and pillage were disgraceful to civilized war. Houses were entered and destroyed in the most wanton manner, and ladies were frightened into handing over jewels and other valuables by threats of violence. He reported that Negro women were ravished in the presence of white women and children. At New Iberia, some of the soldiers obtained some Louisiana rum and caused noise and confusion in the brigade. "These disgusting scenes," he wrote, "were due to the utter incompetency of regimental officers."[9]

Although Banks' troops tried to catch up with Taylor, they were frustrated as they encountered many obstacles. The Union gunboats and transports were prevented from navigating upstream on the Teche because of sunken vessels;

there were long marches along hot, dusty roads; and pontoon bridges had to be constructed where crossings were destroyed—the major project being that of spanning the Vermilion River.

Along the way, Banks ordered the destruction of foundries, the confiscation of livestock and materials, and the tearing down of the buildings and machinery at the Avery Salt mine near New Iberia. Sometime after Banks reached Alexandria, he felt that chasing Taylor across Louisiana was taking up too much time which he wanted to use "more advantageously in another enterprise nearer at hand, and more desirous in its results." No doubt, he meant the reduction of Port Hudson, a goal he had set many months before.[10]

This change of events gave Taylor the opportunity to plunge back into the Bayou Country where he deployed some of his troops and gained an incredible victory in recapturing Brashear City. Although the town was fortified, the Rebels, with around 300 volunteers in a midget fleet composed of skiffs, dugouts, sugar-coolers, flats, etc., consumated a daring attack at dawn on June 23, 1863. This engagement resulted in the capture of the garrison, over a thousand prisoners, and millions of dollars worth of armament and supplies. (As mentioned earlier, details of these dramatic engagments and other action in this specific area can be found in my first book as well as other sources that are listed in the bibliography of this book.)[11]

The battles that occurred in the Bayou Country of Louisiana were unique—quite a contrast to those fought in other parts of the nation. The field of action, in this deep South arena of warfare, usually consisted of bayous, lakes, swamps, marshes, oak-ridges, and sugarcane fields. Armed steamboats, and shallow draft gunboats blasted away at each other in narrow streams while infantry, cavalry and artillery units were engaged in bloody conflicts across the picturesque countryside.

Although the battles of Bisland and Irish Bend were fought on the banks of the Bayou Teche by brave and daring men of the Union and Confederate armies, we must remember that the naval units played a major role in the bloody conflicts as well. The dedicated men who manned the vessels were constantly exposed to the deadly fire from sharpshooters who were hidden along the bayou sides, and, at the same time, faced with the point-blank shelling from the floating fortress in front.

The Union gunboats, which included the *Calhoun, Estrella, Kinsman, Clifton* and *Arizona*, certainly did their part in the campaign and deserved victory. The Confederate gunboats, *Cotton, Queen of the West* and the *Diana*, though outnumbered and outpowered in nearly every engagement, rendered brilliant service to the Confederacy.

The author felt that the performances of the gunboats, officers, and men of both sides didn't get their just play in the history books, and hopes that this rendition may bring to light some of the underlying struggles, sacrifices, and feats of valor.

The author chose to feature the *Diana* because of its dramatic history and legendary activities. It was first a transport, used by the Confederates before it was captured by Farragut's fleet below New Orleans. General Butler placed the boat in operation along the Mississippi River in the transport of troops and supplies, and then had the *Diana* armored and fitted out as a gunboat for the Bayou Country campaign.

Confederates recapture Brashear City in daring attack. (a sketch by the author)

After the Federals captured Berwick Bay and Brashear City, the vessel was utilized in reconnaisances and in the transfer of troops. Later, along with other units of the fleet, it engaged the gunboat *Cotton* up the Atchafalaya River, and was also involved in the ensanguined affair at Cornay's bridge. But in March of 1863, through the negligence and stubbornness of its commander, the vessel and crew were captured by Confederates near Pattersonville where the *Diana* was shattered by gunfire from stem to stern, and the toll of dead and wounded aboard was staggering.

Several weeks later, the gunboat played a starring, but gory role in the Battle of Bisland, as the Confederates courageously used the *Diana* to hold back Banks' powerful forces. This conflict resulted in another bloodbath on board, but this time it was Rebel blood that flowed. The boat took such a pounding that it was forced to retire for repairs. But miraculously, overnight, it was back in action again at the Battle of Irish Bend. Its Parrotts raked the sugarcane field taking its toll of Yankees, and, when it appeared that all was lost, the famous and beloved gunboat was scuttled in the sullen water of Bayou Teche.

The battles in the Bayou Country, especially those that were fought at Bisland and Irish Bend, were not regarded as big battles, but should rank among some of the bloodiest and most intense small battles in American history. The Army and Navy of both sides slugged it out to the bitter end, and, in the midst of it all, a staunch little gunboat by the name of *Diana* was there—and, without a doubt, it was there in all its glory.

THE END

EPILOGUE

The Precious Bell—
A Search for the *Diana*,
And a Mystery is Solved.

Back in the 1940s, while I was employed and living in Franklin, Louisiana, I made the acquaintance of a fine businessman by the name of Pres Gates. I was impressed that he was so well informed on the history of the area and, after several visits with this nice man, I became very interested in the Civil War around Franklin. He told me that sometime after the gunboat *Diana* was scuttled, his grandfather, Alfred Gates, had the bell extracted from the vessel and erected in the belfry of St. Mary's Episcopal Church. Alfred's father was one of the founders of the church, and the church needed a bell.

(In a 1989 Letter to the Editor, which was published in the Episcopal newspaper *Churchwork*, Mrs. Helen Gates Rossner of New Orleans, Pres' sister, wrote about the bell being taken from the *Diana* and that she grew up loving the bell and the church. She stated that after her father died, her sister, Amoret Gates Womack, had the bell reworked. It had clapped for so many years in the same spot that the bell had to be turned and electrified. After 130 years, its reverberating sounds are still heard throughout the city.)

Mr. Gates also told me that there was a book at the library entitled *The 19th Army Corps* by Richard Irwin which gave a generous account of the Teche campaign. I enthusiastically read the book from cover to cover, as my appetite for local Civil War history surged.

While walking through town one day, I heard the clapping of the bell and a strange feeling came over me. I kept thinking that maybe the *Diana* was trying to tell us something, for we were in a period where there were wars, threats of war, racial prejudices, and so forth. It was indeed tragic that so many brave Americans had been killed and wounded aboard the vessel, and I felt that the bell was ringing out a message for the people to strive for peace and unity.

In the year 1970, the Franklin Civic Club sponsored a poetry contest as a highlight of Franklin's Sesquicentennial celebration. I entered the following poem and, much to my delight, it was selected as first place award winner:

THE VOICE OF THE DIANA
(Dedicated to the late Pres Gates of Franklin)

The famous gunboat *Diana*
Which served our country's brave
A century ago was scuttled
And sank to a watery grave.

Her hulk has remained till now
Near the heart of the Parish seat
In the turbid Bayou Teche
At the foot of Willow Street.

The *Diana* was a gallant ship
  Respected for her power;
Her heavy guns and Parrott shells
  Blazed out from the battle tower.

She was first a Union vessel
  Later captured by the Gray,
And left a trail of havoc
  From Franklin to Berwick Bay.

Soldiers fought in bloody conflict
  Along this hallowed shore
But the *Diana* and troops are silent
  They are gone forevermore.

But wait! There is a spark of life
  Which we hope shall never die
For the bell from the *Diana*
  Hangs in a church nearby.

From the Episcopal steeple
  Rings this bell so loud and clear
A miraculous reminder
  Of that tragic yesteryear.

And maybe the bell of the *Diana*
  Which roused the Blue and the Gray
Will become a symbol of unity
  And ring on 'till Judgement Day.

But! Where is the *Diana*? What happened to the
remains? I did know that after the *Diana* was scuttled, Gen.
Banks had the guns shipped to Brashear City and then on to
Algiers (O.R. 15, 728 & 730). For half a century or more,

179

A Gunboat Named Diana

Civil War buffs, treasure seekers, artifact hunters, and engineers have combed the Franklin waterfront and apparently found no evidence of the hull. Area historians were confused as they tried to establish the exact location.

In 1966, the C. S. Thorgeson Contractor of Berwick, Louisiana, while bulkheading the bayou at the foot of Willow Street near the courthouse, pulled two boilers out of the bayou bank and placed them on top of the ground. Thomas Flynn, a geologist and Civil War enthusiast, identified the members as being gunboat boilers. S. W. Poole, a technician from Republic Steel Corporation, confirmed that the plate could well represent 19th century manufacture. This find caused some excitement, and a civic group even proposed to have a small park built around the boilers as a historical memento. But, since no name could be found for positive identification, the project was cancelled. There is a historical marker on the courthouse square which reads in part, "Embedded to the east of this site, and visible from here, are the boilers of the gunboat *Diana*."

I stumbled across a diary written in 1897 by Union Major Thomas McManus of Irish Bend fame, who was revisiting the battlefield and the Bayou Country in general. The major was eating at the O'Niell Hotel which was adjacent to the courthouse, and this is what he wrote:

> Sitting at the dining room window, I looked down at the Bayou Teche on whose banks were the boilers of the old *Queen of the West* which has been lying at the bottom of the lake (meaning Grand Lake) from April 14, 1863 until November, 1895, when the government had caused them to be

raised and removed; they had become a serious obstacle to navigation, having sunk in the mud until they were below the surface of the water.

This brought up another question. Are the boilers those of the *Diana* or *Queen of the West*?

McManus had established many friendships in the Bayou Country including such prominent families as the Fosters, Cafferys, and the O'Niells. In another visit in the year 1907, the major wrote this in his diary right after leaving Senator Don Caffery's home on the north end of the city:

> Just above this place is a monster sugar refinery on the right back of the Teche. The road bends and turns to conform to the bayou windings, on through the village of Teche, near which lies the remains of the old *Diana*. Her boilers and machinery have long since sunk deep in the mud and below the bed of the stream.

Through the efforts of Mrs. H. H. Dinkins, one of the founders of the St. Mary Landmarks Society, an important map was obtained from the Washington, D.C. archives. It was a sketch drawn by E. B. Trinidad in 1870 which shows the approximate location of the scuttled vessel. Trinidad was captain of the U.S. mail steamer *Warren Bell* which made its periodic rounds in the bayou. His map shows the location of 41 stream obstructions. (A partial photo of Trinidad's map is shown in this chapter.)

Interest for finding the gunboat became so intense in 1982 that Franklin Mayor Sam Jones formed a committee for a survey headed by A. J. Hidalgo. A thorough search was conducted, and still, nothing was uncovered. But there was

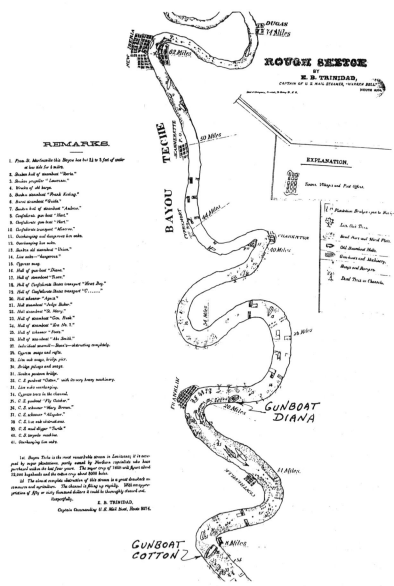

Shown is a portion of Captain Trinidad's 1870 sketch of obstructions in Bayou Teche. (St. Mary Landmarks, Franklin)

good reason that no trace could be found, because the gunboat had long been dismantled and the remnants disposed of.

While lining the drawer of an inherited bureau, Mrs. Routh Trowbridge Wilby ran across a precious bundle of historic papers which included an 1870 survey of Bayou Teche obstructions, and a packet of 62 letter-reports describing the 1871 removal of obstructions. This important find which was made in 1986 puts to rest the longtime question of the "where-abouts" of sunken vessels in the Teche during the Civil War period—and definitely solves the mystery of the legendary *Diana.*

The 1870 survey was authorized by Major C. W. Howell of the U.S. Corps of Engineers, and conducted by William Duke, a civil engineer. Duke's maps show the location of obstructions to navigation which include gunboats, steamboats, sunken rafts, bridge pilings, trees—and even underbrush and snags. The survey extended from St. Martinville to a point west of Patterson where the Teche enters into the Lower Atchafalaya River.

In 1871, the U.S. Corps awarded Daniel Kingsbury a $17,500 contract to remove the obstructions with his crew and wrecking flat, which was called a snagboat and appropriately named *Bayou Teche.*

The removal of the *Diana* took place between April 14 and May 6, 1871. Kingsbury sent periodic letter-reports to Major Howell which gave a good description of the work. The following are some excerpts from those letters which related to the *Diana:*

[April 18th] I find she was heavily ironed with

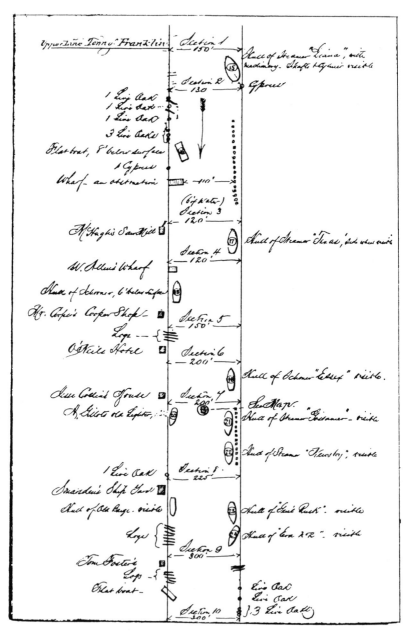

A page from W. D. Duke's survey showing obstructions in Bayou Teche.

plate on her sides, to protect her boilers and machinery. The iron plates are strongly bolted with 1 ¼ inch bolts. I think this part of the *Diana* will require some heavy torpedoes.

[April 24th] We have taken this day the other shaft, portions of the guards, one of the engines and a large shield of timber covered with 23 plates of wrought iron 7'' x 1'' (12 of which are 12 feet 9 inches long.) We have now about 2½ tons wrought iron, and 7 tons cast iron landed on shore.

[May 6th] The wreck of the *Diana* is entirely removed and placed on the left bank of the bayou going up. We made eight blasts, consuming 465 lbs. powder.

In this same letter, Kingsbury mentions the mail boat's Captain Trinidad who was probably an advisor and collaborator in having the obstructions removed:

This evening I start for the wreck of the gunboat *E. J. Hart* which lies about three miles below New Iberia. Capt. Trinidad, master of the steamboat *Iberia,* informs me that the *Hart* is quite an obstruction. If so, I will remove her. Not receiving any instructions from you relative to the old iron taken from the wreck, I have disposed of it to two persons at Franklin to cover expenses.

So there we have it. Maps in this section of the book show the location and position of the *Diana* as well as other vessels during that period. When Major Thomas McManus made

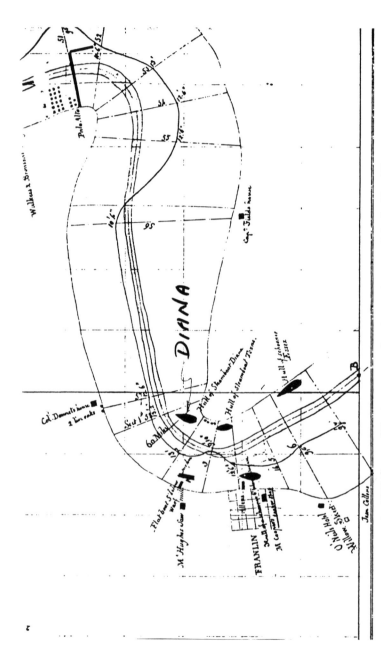

An 1870 Corps of Engineers map showing sunken vessels in the Franklin area.

his visit in 1907, he evidentally saw some bare remnants of the *Diana* lying in the mud.

Mrs. Wilby had her precious findings of letters and maps printed in an attractive book entitled *Clearing Bayou Teche after the Civil War—The Kingsbury Project.* Furthermore, the book is embellished with rare photographs of antebellum homes along the Teche, and some of her fond memories of yesteryear. The book was published by the Center for Louisiana Studies in 1991.

It may be well to mention here that Mrs. Wilby is the granddaughter of the late Murphy Foster who was governor of Louisiana. She and her husband reside at the Dixie Plantation House—the home where she was born, and which is located just east of Franklin.

The Wilbys purchased the antebellum home in 1986. She has returned to the scenes and loves of her childhood—the picturesque countryside, the wildlife, and the quaint Bayou Country lifestyle. She still paddles a pirogue and watches the boats ploughing the waters of the ancient stream.

Routh Wilby made a great contribution to the state and nation by having her historical documents published so that we may all share in her findings. Through her efforts, we learn that the *Diana* is no longer embedded in the banks of Bayou Teche, and Civil War buffs may refrain from their frantic search. I do hope that my book *A Gunboat Named Diana* will enlighten readers with regard to its incredible history, so we may say without reservation, "Yes, the *Diana* is gone, but certainly not forgotten."

Historian Routh Wilby still enjoys paddling her pirogue in Bayou Teche—a sport she began at the age of eleven.

REFERENCES

In the following notes the initials "OR" designate that the information was taken from *The Official Records of the Union and Confederate Armies,* Series 1. The initials "ORN" indicate *The Official Records of the Union and Confederate Navies,* Series 1.

CHAPTER I
THE INVASION

1. Rossiter Johnson, *Campfires and Battlefields,* 88.
2. Richard Irwin, *History of the 19th Army Corps,* 4 & 5.
3. James Parton, *General Butler in New Orleans,* 209.
4. ibid, 220 & 221: Irwin, *History of the 19th Army Corps,* 4 & 5.
5. Parton, *General Butler in New Orleans,* 220.
6. Irwin, *History of the 19th Army Corps,* 10; John Winters, *The Civil War in Louisiana,* 83; ORN, Vol. 18, 280; Johnson, *Campfires and Battlefields,* 90.
7. ibid, 90.
8. Parton, *General Butler in New Orleans,* 223.
9. Benjamin Butler, *Butler's Book,* 361 & 362; ORN, Vol. 18, 263.
10. Irwin, *History of the 19th Army Corps,* 8, 9 & 10.

11. ibid, 5.
12. ibid, 9.
13. Parton, *General Butler in New Orleans,* 210 & 211; Butler, *Butler's Book,* 359 & 362.
14. Parton, *General Butler in New Orleans,* 211; Butler, *Butler's Book,* 359.
15. Parton, *General Butler in New Orleans,* 221.
16. Irwin, *History of the 19th Army Corps,* 12 & 13; Winters, *The Civil War in Louisiana,* 88; Butler, *Butler's Book,* 363.
17. ibid, 363; Parton, *General Butler in New Orleans,* 236; ORN, Vol. 18, 428-430.
18. Butler, *Butler's Book,* 364; Parton, *General Butler in New Orleans,* 236.
19. Butler, *Butler's Book,* 364; Johnson, *Campfires and Battlefields,* 92.
20. ibid; Butler, *Butler's Book,* 364.
21. Johnson, *Campfires and Battlefields,* 92.
22. Butler, *Butler's Book,* 366.
23. Winters, *The Civil War in Louisiana,* 91; ORN, Vol. 18, 154 & 295.
24. Irwin, *History of the 19th Army Corps,* 14.
25. ORN, Vol. 18, 267.
26. ibid, 271.
27. ibid, 297.
28. Irwin, *History of the 19th Army Corps,* 15; Leslie's newsapaper, June 14, 1862, 172.
29. Winters, *The Civil War in Louisiana,* 98; ORN, Vol. 18, 307 & 308.
30. ORN, Vol. 18, 158 & 159.
31. Johnson, *Campfires and Battlefields,* 96.
32. ibid, 96.
33. ORN, Vol. 18, 297.
34. ibid, 761.
35. ibid, 472.

36. Tulane Howard Tilton Library, New Orleans, No. 55-b, Box 43, Vol. 17.
37. *Daily True Delta* newspaper, April 22, 1862; ORN, Vol. 16, 841.
38. ibid, Vol. 16, 841; Enrollment Papers, Washington D.C. Archives, Record Group No. 41; Eldridge Collection, Mariner's Museum, Newport News, Virginia; Library of Congress, Washington, D.C.; Smithsonian Institute, National Museum of American History.
39. ORN, Vol. 18, 710, 723 & 743; Wickham Hoffman, *Camp, Court, and Siege,* 23.

CHAPTER II
YANKEE PENETRATION

1. Ethel Taylor, *Discontent in Confederate Louisiana,* Louisiana History, Vol. II, No. 4, 412.
2. Edwin Davis, *Louisiana, a Narrative Study.*
3. Barnes F. Lathrop, *The Pugh Plantation 1860-1865 (A Study of Life in Lower Louisiana)* 161.
4. ibid, 166 & 167.
5. Richard Taylor, *Destruction and Reconstruction,* 111; Winters, *The Civil War in Louisiana,* 155 & 156.
6. OR, XV, 789 & 919.
7. ibid, 919.
8. ibid; OR VI, Series 2, 814.
9. OR, XV, 426.
10. ibid, 906 & 907.
11. ibid.
12. ibid, 568 & 569.
13. Charles Spurlin, *West of the Mississippi with Waller's 13th Texas Cavalry Battalion,* 2 & 3; Winters, *The Civil War in Louisiana,* 155; Taylor, *Destruction and Reconstruction,* 111.
14. ibid, 112.

15. OR, XV, 133.
16. Spurlin, *West of the Mississippi with Waller,* 48.
17. O'Brien, *Reminiscences of C.C. Cox,* Texas Historical Association Quarterly, 220 & 221.
18. ibid, 222; OR, XV, 133.
19. William Arceneaux, *Acadian General Alfred Mouton,* 53 & 54; Taylor, *Destruction and Reconstruction,* 113; OR, XV, 176.
20. ibid.
21. ibid.
22. Earl Geoghegan, report. National Museum of American History, Smithsonian Institute, Washington, D.C.; J. Thomas Scharf, *Confederate States Navy,* 503; John Fisk Allen, *Memorial for Pickering Dodge Allen,* 103.
23. Routh Trowbridge Wilby, *Clearing Bayou Teche After the Civil War,* 90.
24. Irwin, *History of the 19th Army Corps,* 46.

CHAPTER III
CAPTURE OF BERWICK BAY

1. Irwin, *History of the 19th Army Corps,* 46; OR XV, 166 & 167; Taylor, *Destruction and Reconstruction,* 113; John De Forest, *A Volunteer's Adventure,* 53.
2. ibid, 52.
3. ibid, 55.
4. OR, XV, 176.
5. ibid, 177.
6. ibid.
7. De Forest, *A Volunteer's Adventure,* 56.
8. OR, XV, 178.
9. ibid, 172, 178.
10. ibid, 169.

11. ibid, 159.
12. ORN, Vol. 19, 326, 328 & 333; U.S. Court of Claims #418, 80.
13. ORN, Vol. 19, 326; De Forest, *A Volunteer's Adventure,* 73.
14. ORN, Vol. 19, 330 & 335.
15. ibid, 335.
16. Taylor, *Destruction and Reconstruction,* 119; George Carpenter, *History of the 8th Regiment Vermont Volunteers,* 83; *Attakapas Gazette,* Spring, 1976, Carl Brasseaux, *The Glory Days,* 4 & 7.
17. Carpenter, *History of 8th Vermont,* 82.
18. B.F. Queens' report, *Franklin Banner Tribune* Historical, April 28, 1959; ORN, Series II, Vol. 1, 251.
19. ORN, Vol. 19, 327.
20. ibid.
21. David Edmonds, *Yankee Autumn in Acadiana,* 10; Governeur Morris, *History of a Volunteer Regiment,* 92 & 93.
22. OR, XV, 170 & 184; Carpenter's, *History of the 8th Vermont,* 71.
23. OR, XV, 170, 171 & 172.
24. ibid, 162 & 171.
25. ORN, Vol. 19, 332.

CHAPTER IV
THE STRIFE AT CORNAY'S BRIDGE

1. OR, XV, 179 & 180; Taylor, *Destruction and Reconstruction,* 120; ORN, Vol. 19, 328.
2. Irwin, *History of the 19th Army Corps,* 94; Taylor, *Destruction and Reconstruction,* 120; OR, 15, 179 & 180.
3. Irwin, *History of the 19th Army Corps,* 94; Taylor, *Destruction and Reconstruction,* 121.
4. ORN, Vol. 19, 327 & 328.

5. ibid.

6. ORN, Vol. 19, 327 & 623; Smithsonian Institute.

7. ORN, Vol. 19, 332 & 333.

8. ibid, 336.

9. ibid, 328.

10. OR, XV, 184 & 185.

11. ORN, Vol. 19, 334 & 337.

12. ibid, 336 & 337.

13. ibid, 329.

14. ibid, 328.

15. French and American Claims Commission, U.S. Court of Claims, 1883, No. 418, 89.

16. ORN, Vol. 19, 328.

17. Irwin, *History of the 19th Army Corps,* 48 & 49.

CHAPTER V

THE FATE OF THE *COTTON*

1. Taylor, *Destruction and Reconstruction,* 114; brochure, *History of the Avery Island Saltmine.*

2. *The Daily Southern Crisis,* Jackson, Mississippi, Jan. 24, 1863.

3. OR, XV, 1088.

4. ibid.

5. Report by Mobil Oil geologist (1965).

6. *The Daily Southern Crisis,* Jackson, Mississippi, Jan. 24, 1863.

7. OR, XV, 590; Irwin, *History of the 19th Army Corps,* 54 & 55; T. Michael Parrish, *Richard Taylor,* 171-180; Clement Evans, *Confederate Military History of Louisiana,* 88.

8. ibid.

9. ORN, Vol. 19, 494 & 495.

10. Irwin, *History of the 19th Army Corps,* 62, 63, & 64.

11. ORN, Vol. 19, 393.
12. ibid, 394.
13. Evans, *Confederate Military History of Louisiana,* 82; Irwin, *History of the 19th Army Corps,* 73; OR, XV, 234-237.
14. ibid, 234; ORN, Vol. 19, 518; Irwin, *History of the 19th Army Corps,* 73; John Stanyan, *History of the 8th Regiment New Hampshire Vols.,* 162 & 163.
15. Taylor, *Destruction and Reconstruction,* 120 & 121; Stanyan, *History of the 8th Regiment New Hampshire Vols.,* 163.
16. ORN, Vol. 19, 518.
17. ibid, 522.
18. ibid, 516, 518, & 519; Winters, *The Civil War in Louisiana,* 212 & 213.
19. ORN, Vol. 19, 520.
20. ibid, 522-524; Winters, *The Civil War in Louisiana,* 213; *Houston Tri-Weekly Telegraph,* February 2, 1863.
21. ORN, Vol. 19, 524; Carl Brasseaux, *Attakapas Gazette,* Spring 1976, 13 & 14.
22. John Stanyan, *History of the 8th Regiment New Hampshire Vols.,* 163.
23. OR, XV, 234 & 235.
24. Stanyan, *History of the 8th Regiment, New Hampshire Vols.,* 165 & 166; Letter from John Parkerson, March 12, 1976.
25. Brasseaux, *Attakapas Gazette,* Spring 1976, 14.

CHAPTER VI
CAPTURE OF THE *DIANA*

1. OR, XV, 240 & 241.
2. ibid.
3. ibid, 242; ORN, Vol. 19, 617.
4. OR, XV, 244.

5. ibid, 245; Irwin, *History of the 19th Army Corps,* 86 & 87; ORN, Vol. 19, 611.
6. OR, XV, 680, 681, 1105, 1107 & 1108.
7. ibid, 819; Jerry Thompson, *Henry Hopkins Sibley,* preface.
8. OR, XV, 680, 681, 1105, 1107 & 1108.
9. Dr. Harris Beecher, *Record of the 114th New York, Vols.,* 120; ORN, Vol. 19, 624, 625, & 626.
10. Winters, *The Civil War in Louisiana,* 221.
11. ORN, Vol. 19, 640.
12. A.J. Duganne, *20 Months in the Dept. of the Gulf,* 195.
13. ibid, 195 & 196.
14. John Fisk Allen, *Memorial of Pickering Dodge Allen,* 98.
15. ibid, 93 & 98.
16. Duganne, *20 Months in the Dept. of the Gulf,* 196, 197 &198; George O'Brien's, *Reminiscences of C.C. Cox,* 22 & 23 (Texas Historical Society); Allen, *Memorial of Pickering Dodge Allen,* 98 & 99.
17. Duganne, *20 Months in the Dept. of the Gulf,* 197 & 198.
18. ibid, 198.
19. Allen, *Memorial of Pickering Dodge Allen,* 98 & 99.
20. ibid.
21. Ibid.
22. Duganne, *20 Months in the Dept. of the Gulf,* 199-201.
23. ibid, 201.
24. ibid.
25. ibid, 102.
26. ORN, Vol. 20, 109 & 113.
27. ibid, 113.
28. ibid, 109 & 110.

29. ibid, 112 & 113; Frank Flinn, *Campaigning with Banks and Sheridan,* 32.
30. ibid; ORN, Vol. 20, 113.
31. ORN, Vol. 19, 699.
32. Allen, *Memorial of Pickering Dodge Allen,* 112, 145 & 146.
33. ibid, 145 & 146.

CHAPTER VII
BISLAND

1. Beecher, *Record of the 114th New York Volunteers,* 126 & 128.
2. ibid, 129; James Hall, *Cayuga in the Field,* 89.
3. ibid.
4. Beecher, *Record of the 114th New York Volunteers,* 129 & 130.
5. ibid, 131; Duganne, *20 Months in the Dept. of the Gulf,* 157; William Tiemann, *159th Regiment of the New York State Vols.,* 27.
6. Beecher, *Record of the 114th New York Vols.,* 133.
7. Hall, *Cayuga in the Field,* 90; OR, XV, 386; Theo. Noel, *Campaign from Santa Fe to the Mississippi,* 71.
8. OR, XV, 294; Beecher, *Record of the 114th New York Vols.,* 134 & 135.
9. Irwin, *History of the 19th Army Corps,* 91; Beecher, *Record of the 114th New York Vols.,* 137; OR, XV, 358.
10. Frank Moore, *Rebellion Record,* 529; Flinn, *Campaigning with Banks and Sheridan,* 33 & 34.
11. OR, XV, 388.
12. ibid, 396 & 397.
13. Flinn, *Campaigning with Banks and Sheridan,* 37.
14. ibid, 40; Moore, *Rebellion Record,* 531.
15. OR, XV, 388 & 389.
16. ibid.
17. ibid.

18. Winters, *The Civil War in Louisiana,* 224.
19. James Ewer, *3rd Massachusetts Cavalry,* 70; OR, XV, 358.
20. ibid, 389.
21. Flinn, *Campaigning with Banks and Sheridan,* 41.
22. Moore, *Rebellion Record,* 532; Flinn, *Campaigning with Banks and Sheridan,* 42.
23. ibid, 41 & 42.
24. Beecher, *Record of the 114th New York Vols.,* 141 & 142; Moore, *Rebellion Record,* 533; Flinn, *Campaigning with Banks and Sheridan,* 42.
25. OR, XV, 390.
26. Beecher, *Record of the 114th New York Vols.,* 142; Moore, *Rebellion Record,* 533; Flinn, *Campaigning with Banks and Sheridan,* 42.
27. ibid, 41, 42, 43, & 44.
28. Colonel Tom Ochiltree's article, *San Francisco Examiner,* October 7, 1888, 12.
29. ibid.
30. OR, XV, 340.
31. ibid.
32. Flinn, *Campaigning with Banks and Sheridan,* 44-46; OR, XV, 390.
33. Ochiltree, *San Francisco Examiner,* October 7, 1888, 12.
34. Flinn, *Campaigning with Banks and Sheridan,* 53 & 54; OR, XV, 347.
35. Irwin, *History of the 19th Army Corps,* 100.
36. ibid.
37. Taylor, *Destruction and Reconstruction,* 132 & 133.
38. ibid.

CHAPTER VIII
IRISH BEND

1. OR, XV, 386.
2. ORN, Vol. 20, 134 & 135.

3. OR, XV, 358 & 359; Cecil Eby, *A Virginia Yankee in the Civil War,* 169.
4. OR, XV, 358.
5. Irwin, *History of the 19th Army Corps,* 106.
6. ibid; OR, XV, 358, 359, 364 & 371.
7. ibid, 363, 364, 377 & 381; Moore, *Rebellion Record,* Vol. VI, 544; Irwin, *History of the 19th Army Corps,* 105 & 106.
8. OR, XV, 359.
9. Moore, *Rebellion Record,* Vol. VI, 540; Irwin, *History of the 19th Army Corps,* 107; OR, XV, 359.
10. OR, VIII, Chapter 66, 466.
11. OR, XV, 359; OR, VIII, Chapter 66, 466.
12. Irwin, *History of the 19th Army Corps,* 108; Homer Sprague, *History of the 13th Connecticut Vols.,* 110; James Hosmer, *The Color Guard,* 129.
13. Sprague, *History of the 13th Connecticut Vols.,* 110; J.F. Moors, *History of the 52nd Massachusetts Regiment,* 116; Hosmer, *The Color Guard,* 129 & 130; Mrs. Thomas Holmes, *Oaklawn Manor.*
14. Irwin, *History of the 19th Army Corps,* 112; Holmes, *Oaklawn Manor.*
15. OR, XV, 390, 391, 392; Tiemann, *159th Regiment of the New York State Vols.,* 29.
16. Taylor, *Destruction and Reconstruction,* 132 & 133.
17. Irwin, *History of the 19th Army Corps,* 109 & 110; Sprague, *History of the 13th Connecticut Vols.,* 111.
18. Moore, *Rebellion Record,* VI, 544; Thomas McManus, *25th Connecticut Vols.,* 36 & 37; Tiemann, *159th Regiment of the New York State Vols.,* 28-30.
19. Moore, *Rebellion Record,* VI, 545; McManus, *25th Connecticut Vols.,* 37.
20. ibid.
21. Moore, *Rebellion Record,* VI, 545.
22. Sprague, *History of the 13th Connecticut Vols.,* 113;

Tiemann, *159th Regiment of the New York State Vols.,* 29, 30 & 82.

23. ibid, 82.
24. ibid, 29; Sprague, *History of the 13th Connecticut Vols.,* 115; McManus, *25th Connecticut Vols.,* 38.
25. ibid; Sprague, *History of the 13th Connecticut,* 118.
26. OR, XV, 392, 393 & 395.
27. Elden Maddocks, *History of the 26th Maine,* 29 & 32; McManus, *25th Connecticut Vols.,* 38.
28. OR, XV, 392.
29. Irwin, *History of the 19th Army Corps,* 101.
30. OR, VIII, Chapter 66, 464 & 465.
31. OR, XV, 392 & 393.
32. ibid, 392 & 399; Irwin, *History of the 19th Army Corps,* 115; Beecher, *Record of the 114th New York Vols.,* 152; Taylor, *Destruction and Reconstruction,* 134; *Planters Banner,* Franklin, LA, April 26, 1871.
33. Ewer, *3rd Massachusetts Cavalry,* 74.
34. Taylor, *Destruction and Reconstruction,* 74, 76 & 134; Irwin, *History of the 19th Army Corps,* 115 & 116; Stanyan, *History of the 8th Regiment New Hampshire Vols.,* 204.
35. Irwin, *History of the 19th Army Corps,* 115 & 116.
36. Sprague, *History of the 13th Connecticut Vols.,* 120.
37. Interview with M.C. Rose of Franklin, LA; Hosmer, *The Color Guard,* 135.
38. Moore, *Rebellion Record,* Vol. VI, 546.

CHAPTER IX

THE DEMISE OF THE *QUEEN*

1. Irwin, *History of the 19th Army Corps,* 121; ORN, Vol. 20, 134, 135, 137 & 138.
2. Scharf, *Confederate States Navy,* 351 & 352.
3. ORN, Vol. 20, 137 & 138; Irwin, *History of the 19th Army Corps,* 121 & 122; Scharf, *Confederate States Navy,* Vol. 1, 363.

4. ibid.
5. *Richmond Sentinel,* June 24, 1863; Taylor, *Destruction and Reconstruction,* 135; Harry Wright Newman, *The Maryland Semmes and Kindred Families,* 92 & 93.
6. Ewer, *3rd Massachusetts Cavalry,* 74.
7. Beecher, *Record of the 114th New York Vols.,* 152; Duganne, *20 Months in the Dept. of the Gulf,* 103.
8. Irwin, *History of the 19th Army Corps,* 116.
9. OR, XV, 373.
10. ibid, 313.
11. Taylor, *Destruction and Reconstruction,* 141; Duganne, *20 Months in the Dept. of the Gulf,* 143 & 144; Noel, *A Campaign from Santa Fe to the Mississippi,* 82 & 83.

A SELECTED BIBLIOGRAPHY

BOOKS

Arceneaux, William. *Acadian General Alfred Mouton and the Civil War,* Lafayette, LA: University of Southwestern Louisiana, 1981.

Beecher, Harris H. *History of the 114th Regiment, NYSV.* Norwich, NY: I.F. Hubbard, 1866.

Butler, Benjamin. *Butler's Book.* Boston, MA: A.M. Thayer & Co., 1892.

Carpenter, George N. *History of the Eighth Vermont Volunteers 1861-1865.* Boston, MA: Press of Deland and Barta, 1886.

Davis, Edwin Adams. *Louisiana, a Narrative Study.* New Orleans, LA: J.F. Hayer Publishing Co., 1960.

DeForest, John William. *A Volunteer's Adventures: A Union Captain's Record of the Civil War.* New Haven, CT: Yale University Press, 1946.

Duganne, A.J.H. *Camps and Prisons; Twenty Months in the Department of the Gulf.* New York, NY: 1865.

Eby, Jr., Cecil D. *A Virginia Yankee in the Civil War; The Diaries of David Hunter Strother.* Chapel Hill, NC: The University of North Carolina Press, 1961.

Edmonds, David C. *Yankee Autumn in Acadiana.* Lafayette, LA: The Acadiana Press, 1979.

Ewer, James K. *The Third Massachusetts Cavalry in the War for the Union.* Boston, MA: Historical Committee of the Regimental Association, 1903.

Flinn, Frank M. *Campaigning with Banks in Louisiana, '63 and '64, and with Sheridan in the Shenandoah Valley in '64 and '65.* Lynn, MA: Press of Thomas P. Nichols, 1887.

Hall, James. *Cayuga in the Field. A Record of the 75th New York Volunteers.* Auburn, NY, 1873.

Hoffman, Wickham. *Camp, Court, and Siege, a Narrative of Personal Adventure and Observation During Two Wars, 1861-1865 and 1870-1871.* New York, NY: Harper & Brothers, 1877.

Hosmer, James K. *The Color Guard.* Boston, MA: Walker, Wise and Co., 1864.

Irwin, Richard B. *History of the Nineteenth Army Corps.* New York, NY: G.P. Putnam's Sons, 1893.

Johnson, Rossiter. *Campfires and Battlefields.* New York, NY: The Blue and Grey Press, 1958.

Maddocks, Elden B. *History of the Twenty-Sixth Maine Regiment.* Bangor, ME: Charles H. Glass & Co., 1899.

McManus, Thomas (co-authors: Colonel George Bissell, Samuel Ellis, and Lt. Henry Hill Goodell). *The Twenty-Fifth Regiment of Connecticut Volunteers.* Rockville, CT: Press of the Rockville Journal, 1913.

Moore, Frank. *The Rebellion Record: A Diary of American Events.* New York, NY: D. Van Norstrand, 1865.

Moors, J.F. *History of the Fifty-Second Regiment Massa-

chusetts Volunteers. Boston, MA: George Ellis Press, 1893.

Morris, Gouverneur. *The History of a Volunteer Regiment.* New York, NY: Veteran Volunteer Publishing Co., 1891.

Noel, Theophilus. *A Campaign from Santa Fe to the Mississippi.* Houston, Texas: Stagecoach Press, 1961.

Parton, James. *General Butler in New Orleans.* New York, NY: Mason Brothers, 1864.

Scharf, J. Thomas. *Confederate States Navy from its Organization to the Surrender of its Last Vessel.* San Francisco and New York, 1887.

Sprague, Homer B. *History of the 13th Infantry Regiment of Connecticut Volunteers.* Hartford, CT: Case, Lockwood and Co., 1867.

Spurlin, Charles, ed. *West of the Mississippi with Waller's 13th Texas Cavalry Battalion.* Hillsboro, Texas: Hill Junior College, 1971.

Stanyan, John M. *A History of the Eighth Regiment of New Hampshire Volunteers.* Concord, NH: Ira C. Evans, printer, 1892.

Taylor, Richard. *Destruction and Reconstruction.* New York, NY: D. Appleton and Co., 1897.

Thompson, Jerry. *Henry Hopkins Sibley: Confederate General of the West.* Natchitoches, LA: Northwestern State University Press, 1987.

Tiemann, William F. *The 159th Regiment Infantry, New York State Volunteers.* Brooklyn, NY: Published by Tiemann, 1891.

(Secretary of War) *War of the Rebellion, Official Records of the Union and Confederate Armies.* Washington, D.C.: Government Printing Office, 1880-1901.

(Secretary of War) *War of the Rebellion, Official Records of the Union and Confederate Armies.* Washington, D.C.: Government Printing Office, 1894-1922.

Winters, John D. *The Civil War in Louisiana:* The Louisiana State University Press, 1963.

Wilby, Routh Trowbridge. *Clearing Bayou Teche after the Civil War—The Kingsbury Project, 1870-1871.* Lafayette, LA: Center for Louisiana Studies, University of Southwestern Louisiana, 1991.

NEWSPAPERS and other PERIODICALS

Attakapas Gazette, Lafayette, LA.
Daily Southern Crisis, Jackson, MS.
Daily True Delta, New Orleans, LA.
Franklin Banner Tribune, Franklin, LA.
Harper's Weekly, New York, NY.
Leslie's Illustrated Weekly, New York, NY.
Louisiana Historical Quarterly Journal, Lafayette, LA.
Pierce County Herald, Ellsworth, WI.
Planter's Banner, Franklin, LA.
Richmond Sentinel, Richmond, VA.
San Francisco Examiner, San Francisco, CA.
Tri-Weekly, Houston, TX.

DIARIES, NARRATIVES, PAPERS and other SOURCES

Articles relative to the 4th Wisconsin Infantry Regiment, Madison, WI: State Historical Society of Wisconsin.

Avery Island Saltmine, historical article (brochure).

Bennet, Lucian B. Memoir. Ellsworth, WI: *Pierce County Herald,* 1965.

Brasseux, Carl. ed. *The Glory Days. E.T. King Recalls the Civil War Years.* Lafayette, LA: Attakapas Historical Association (*Attakapas Gazette*), Spring, 1976.

Confederate Naval Museum, Columbus, GA. Letter relative to the *Diana,* 1981.

Eldridge Collection, Mariner's Museum, Newport News, VA.

Enrollment papers for the *Diana.* Port of Pittsburgh. November 3rd, 1858. (National Archives)

French and American Claims Commission, U.S. Court of Claims, Washington, D.C., 1883.

Geoghegan, Earl. Report on the *Diana.* National Museum of American History, Smithsonian Institute, Washington, D.C.

Langley, Harold D., Curator, National Museum of American History. Papers relative to the *Diana.* January 22, 1988.

Latrop, Barnes, F. *The Pugh Plantation,* 1860-1865.

Library of Congress, Washington, D.C.

The Mariner's Museum, Newport News, VA, *Merchant Steam Vessels of the U.S.,* 1790-1868.

Molineux, Col. Edward. Papers and letters, 1863 & 1864. Williamsburg, VA.

O'Brien, George. *Reminiscences of C.C. Cox.:* Texas Historical Association Quarterly, 1903.

Ochiltree, Tom. *A Famous Fighter.* An article on Judge Ed McGowan, San Francisco, CA: *San Francisco Examiner,* October 7, 1888.

Parkerson, John. Letter recalling his great-grandmother's experience during the Civil War. March 12, 1976.

Queens, B.F. Report. *Franklin Banner Tribune Historical,* April 28, 1959.

Rose, M.C. Interview relative to Irish Bend Civil War burial, 1993.

Rossner, Helen Gates. New Orleans, LA. Letter relative to the *Diana,* 1989.

Taylor, Ethel. *Discontent in Confederate Louisiana.* Louisiana History, Vol. II, No. 4.

University of Texas at Austin. Steamboats and newspaper index entries; Houston Navagation Company.

INDEX

214

Index